HAPPY EASTER
t B BARRETT
FROM
AUNT OSIE

HAVE FUN!

THE PARTY BOOK

FOR BOYS AND GIRLS

Bernice Wells Carlson

THE PARTY BOOK

FOR BOYS AND GIRLS

Illustrated by Faith C. Minnerly

New York ABINGDON Nashville

To Christine, Paul, Philip, and Marta

I should like to thank the many people who have helped with the preparation of this book, especially Mrs. D. S. Wilt and Cub Scouts of Pack 171, Den 10, Westfield, New Jersey; Mrs. Madison Weidner and Girl Scouts of Troop 214, Middlebush, New Jersey; David Ginglend, teacher, Lincoln School, Plainfield, New Jersey; Mrs. Harry S. Layton, New Jersey Conference Secretary of Christian Social Relations, The Methodist Church; Mrs. Paul Wigg, Pontiac, Michigan; Mrs. Eugene Howe, Somerset, New Jersey; my children, Christine and Philip; and my husband, Dr. Carl W. Carlson.

CONTENTS

PLAN A PARTY

Most parties are fun, but some are more fun than others. Why? The reason is good planning. Some parties are planned better than others.

This book is full of well-planned parties. If you give a party like one described here, you and your guests will have a good time. Or you may enjoy planning an original party, based on suggestions given in this book.

This is a children's party book, a book which tells boys and girls how they can start when they are very young to help with their own parties; how they can take more responsibility when they are a little older; and how, after a time, they can give their own parties—with the consent, advice, and usually the help of an adult who may serve as a referee, cook, or at least as an interested observer.

This book can be used by one person giving a party in his own home; by two or more boys and girls giving a party together; or by a group of boys and girls, such as a troop or class, giving a party at their meeting place.

HOW TO USE THIS BOOK

Each chapter in this book suggests one way that you can give a party or help a younger child give one. There are games you can play; refreshments you may want to serve; and invitations, decorations, and favors you can make.

The directions for the games and other activities are specific, and the instructions for handicraft are accurate. But the ideas in this book are only suggestions. You must use good judgment when you make plans for your own party. You know what your friends like to play. You know what space you have. You know what favors your friends like. Change these plans to fit your needs. Or make a completely new set of plans for your own party, using general suggestions given in this book.

WHEN TO GIVE A PARTY

Any time is a good time for a party. You do not need to wait for Halloween, Christmas, or a birthday. In fact, sometimes it is more fun not to have a party right on a birthday. Some boys and girls who have winter birthdays prefer to give parties in the summer when guests can play out of doors. Some boys and girls with summer birthdays like to have parties in the spring or fall; because too many of their friends are out of town during the vacation months. Brownies, Cubs, Scouts, or other youth groups can turn a meeting into a party with a theme.

You can entertain for other people. Introduce the new girl in the neighborhood, say goodbye to the boy who is moving away, honor someone's cousins who are visiting in your neighborhood. You can give a party just for the fun of it. But whenever you ask people to come to your home, be sure to plan in advance what they are to do.

GETTING HELP

Giving your own party does not mean giving a party all by yourself. No one does that unless he lives alone. First of all get permission to have a party. If the party is to be at home, discuss your plans with your parents. If you belong to a club, discuss the plans with your advisor. Decide when to have the party, in what rooms to give it, and how many people to invite. Plan together what games to play and decide who will introduce the games and referee them. Agree on what food to serve and how to serve it.

A PARTY THEME

Having a theme adds fun to a party. It gives you a chance to use your imagination and helps you tie different parts of a party together, making it one continuous event. For example, you may decide on an Indian theme. What Indian invitations and favors can you make? How can you change the games you know into Indian games? What can you call everyday food to make it seem like Indian food? As you can see, a theme turns a party, even a very small party, into a special event —rather than just another playtime followed by ice cream and cake.

When you choose a theme, consider the place in which you will give the party. For example, you can give an indoor cowboy party, but somehow cowboys make you think of the great out-of-doors. It might be a good idea to choose some other theme for a winter party, and save the cowboy party for a time of year when you can play out-of-doors.

WHOM TO INVITE

Invite your friends to your party, the boys and girls with whom you ordinarily play. Choose guests who are very close to your own age in order to have nearly equal competition in games. If you are eight years old and your twelve-year-old neighbor often plays with you, ask her to come to help with games.

Children of different ages like to do different things and have different abilities. A twelve-year-old doesn't want to play LONDON BRIDGE unless she is helping younger children play. A four-year-old child can't play word games or spelling games, and will always be IT in a game of tag, if he is playing with eight-year-olds.

HOW MANY TO INVITE

Keep your parties small, especially when you are playing indoors. Many games require only six or eight players, including yourself. Don't try to entertain more than twelve guests even if you have a large recreation room in which to play.

The more guests you have, the more help you will need in directing games and other activities. Don't hesitate to ask for help. If you are playing outdoors, with eight or more guests, ask an adult to direct activities and referee.

INVITATIONS

You do not need to send invitations, but they can be fun to make and are fun to receive. And, they show the date, time, and place of the party so that there is no misunderstanding about when to arrive— and when to go home!

Always put "R.S.V.P." on your invitations. This stands for the French phrase, "Answer, if you please." Always answer an invitation, even if it does not say "R.S.V.P." A host must know how many guests are coming in order to make plans.

TIME OF THE PARTY

As a rule, two hours are enough time for any party. Often an hour and a half is plenty. Discuss with your parents or advisors the best time to have a party. You can have a morning party and finish with a regular lunch. Or you can start with dessert, either in the afternoon or early evening, and then have games and other activities. Or you can have a late afternoon party, followed by a simple supper; or an early evening party, ending with light refreshments.

Think of the time of day when you are planning activities. During the summer it is best to be quiet during the heat of the day. If you plan any kind of treasure or scavenger hunt, be sure that players return to the scene of the party before dark.

PLANNING PARTY GAMES

Keep in mind the following suggestions in choosing games.

Start with some loosely organized activity. Guests seldom arrive at the same time. Suggest that they do something that will encourage them to talk to one another as they are waiting for later arrivals.

Alternate quiet and active games so that no one will get too tired. There are active games you can play in a small room. For example, guests must not run a regular relay race in a living room; but they can waddle like ducks in a relay race anywhere.

Include games for everyone. Have games testing physical skill and games testing mental skill, games that are won by chance, and games in which players take turns being IT. Be sure that everyone has a chance to be IT; or if the party is a large club party, that no one is IT again and again.

Have guests work in teams, or at least as couples, whenever possible. This is an especially good idea when playing any type of puzzle, riddle, or "figure it out" game. One person helps another, and no one is ashamed because he was the last to think of something.

Include games that can be played as long as guests are interested, such as circle games, try-to-find-it games, dramatic games, marching, or handicraft fun. If you have nothing but races, your party may be over before you know it. It is impossible to time a party exactly, saying that this race will take so many minutes and that game so long.

Be reasonably inactive before eating. Story games, handicraft, dancing, or marching are all good before-we-eat activities.

Try to include some activities which encourage players to use their imaginations. In every chapter in this book there is some activity that encourages guests to be creative; a story game, handicraft, a dramatic game, or a use-your-imagination situation.

Depend on games which everyone knows, using your own variations to fit your theme. For example, almost everyone knows the game in which IT closes his eyes, turns around, and points to SOMEONE. SOMEONE makes a sound and IT tries to guess his identity. SOMEONE may *moo* like a cow at a Farmer's Party, sing a carol at a Christmas Party, or yell like an Indian at an Indian Party. Stunts may be new. Be prepared to demonstrate them. Either your guests can do them or they can't. The fun is in trying. Never introduce more than one really new game at a party. Avoid difficult games.

Don't play games which require waiting a long time for a turn. For example, if you plan to have people pitch bean bags into a basket, limit the number of players to three or four, giving each player two tosses at one turn. One solution for this type of play is to have several contests in progress at the same time, with players going from game to game.

It is all right to ask players to take turns for stunt contests, such as two people trying to wrap a package with one hand each. Stunt contests are as much fun to watch as to perform.

Avoid drop-out games that take a long time for elimination. First-person-out grows tired of watching others. If you play a variation of GOING TO JERUSALEM with a fairly large group, have two players withdraw chairs at a time. The real contest starts when only two chairs remain and three players remain in the game. This is fun to watch— but the one-by-one elimination can be boring.

Plan an extra game to use if there is extra time. It is better to plan too much to do than too little.

DIRECTING GAMES

Always ask an adult to attend your party. Decide before the party just what activities you will direct and when you want the adult to help you. When there is a contest, always ask the adult to referee.

Be sure that you understand every game and every contest. Convince your guests that there is one set of rules and everyone will follow these at the party. (Many games are old, old games, and rules differ slightly when played by different people in different places.)

If a game or stunt is new or difficult, practice it before the party or play it with your family.

When introducing a new game or stunt contest, demonstrate it and let guests practice it before the contest. For example, in pass the orange from chin to chin, show how to hold an orange under your chin and let guests pass it down the line without racing. In a rabbit relay, let guests hop a few minutes before racing. If a circle game, or other formation game, is new, ask players to walk through it before they play it.

Make a list of party activities. Don't trust your memory. In the party excitement, you may forget what you had planned.

If you discover that some activity doesn't "click" with your guests, forget it. Don't get upset or complain. Stay happy and go on to the next activity.

If guests like a game especially well, repeat it, or play it longer than you had originally planned, even if it means omitting another game. However, stop playing a game before guests tire of it.

Use a whistle when you need it to get the attention of players.

BEING HOST OR HOSTESS

If a party is given at your home, you are the host or hostess. You should greet every guest at the door and take his coat or sweater, if he is wearing one. Make sure that he knows everyone and see to it that he is included in all activities. It is up to you to try to make everyone happy and at ease.

You must help with every game and activity in one way or another. You may introduce a game, or you may demonstrate how to play it, or you may help pass out equipment. Whatever has to be done, you must be on hand to do it.

When the party is over, you should say good-bye to your guests, and let them know you are happy they could come.

A PRESCHOOL PARTY

A party for a preschool brother or sister is different in certain ways from your own party. Keep it very small, very simple, and shorter than a party for an older child.

Little children often play side by side, each with his own truck or doll, rather than playing together. This is natural. Don't try to force them to join in group activity if they are not ready for it.

You can encourage them to play simple song and circle games, such as RING AROUND THE ROSIE or DID YOU EVER SEE A LASSIE? Very young children usually like these games. However, if one of the children doesn't want to join the group, let him watch the others play.

Little children are not ready for strenuous competition. Never put great emphasis on winning and never give a valuable prize to one child. The others are sure to feel neglected. If you play a simple contest game, like PIN THE TAIL ON THE DONKEY, ask "Who got the tail closest to the right spot? Tom did. Good for Tom!" Pat him on the back. That is reward enough.

Try to have a preschool party in the morning when children are the least tired. Always have at least one mother or teacher helping at a preschool party.

A BIRTHDAY PARTY

The parties in the book are not birthday parties, but you may use one for a birthday party if you wish. You will be the host as well as guest of honor.

Preschool children usually like to open gifts the minute they receive them. They may be willing to allow the guests to play with the new toys, and they may not. You may find a guest who doesn't want to give away the gift he brought. Don't get upset. Ask your adult helper to solve the problem.

Older boys and girls usually like to open gifts near the close of the party.

Some boys and girls celebrate their birthdays by bringing refreshments to school or to a troop meeting. Of course, your teacher or your troop leader must agree to the plan if you want to celebrate your birthday party this way.

A CLUB PARTY

A party for an organized group is very much like a party given at home. Use the same basic rules for planning: a get-acquainted period, followed by active and quiet games and other activities. Select games and other activities which members can play and like to play. Offer a variety of games so that everyone can excel or win by chance.

A club party must have a chairman, or a committee and a chairman. Although the chairman may be a leader and introduce games and direct them, an adult advisor must be on hand to referee. An advisor may want to direct all activities so that all club members can take part.

LET'S GO TO A ——— PARTY

Boys and girls of the middle age group frequently entertain a few friends by taking them to some special place: a football game, a baseball game, a children's theater production, a movie that is good for children, the aquarium, the zoo, and so on. Any visit that would interest you probably would interest your very best friends.

These visits require special planning. In some cases your parents must get tickets in advance, and they must always plan for transportation. Sometimes you can serve refreshments at home, before the show or game, especially if you have reserved seats. If you must go to a game early in order to get seats, take along paper-bag lunches for your guests and buy soft drinks at the game. If you are going to the zoo, plan to have a picnic lunch in a park.

So plan your party. Then have fun! A well-planned party is a *good* party—fun for you and fun for your guests.

LET'S-PRETEND-WE'RE-LADIES PARTY

"Dried beans are funny," remarked Laura Blake as she opened a package of dry limas for her mother. "Every bean is different."

"Just like faces," suggested her mother.

"That's right," said Laura, picking up a bean and looking at it carefully. "Turn one this way and you have a fat face. Turn it this way and you have a long face. That gives me an idea! May I have some beans?"

"Of course," answered her mother, without asking, "What for?"

A little later, Laura got out her "What's-in-it?" box, which held an odd assortment of broken strings of beads, bits of feathers, discarded fabric corsages, stones from old costume jewelry—anything that Laura thought was pretty and small enough to fit into the box. She also assembled some used ribbon, scraps of yarn, net, and cloth. Her equipment included tweezers and pins which she could use to push tiny bits of yarn or ribbon just where she wanted them to go.

Using beans as faces, she designed the heads and shoulders of ladies of fashion and glued them onto filing cards. Sure enough! Each face was different, and each lady wore a different hat and different blouse.

"How adorable!" said Mrs. Blake as she looked at the cards.

"Mother, may I have a Let's-Pretend-We're-Ladies Party? We could dress up like ladies, eat at card tables, maybe play a table game—we could use these for place cards." Laura was getting many ideas, not necessarily in order.

"Sounds like fun," said Mrs. Blake.

"What can I use for invitations? What else looks like a face, besides a lima bean?" asked Laura.

"How about a button?" suggested Mrs. Blake.

"Oh, yes, I'll make ladies with long dresses and button faces."

Laura, with her mother's help, planned a guest list. Then Laura made button-faced-lady invitations (page 28). "Let's Pretend We're Ladies. Bring a dress to dress up in," she wrote beneath the picture and added the date, time and place of party, and her name.

"This is one party I don't want to miss," remarked Mr. Blake as he listened to Laura's plans and pictured her little friends dressed in old formals and teetering about in high-heeled shoes. "Isn't there something you want me to do?"

"Would you be an official photographer, Daddy? Would you?" pleaded Laura. "We'd really like to have pictures."

"Would I?" laughed Mr. Blake. "I should welcome the opportunity," he continued, pretending to be businesslike. "I'll take pictures the ladies will cherish forever."

"Planning a party is as much fun as giving one," sang Laura as she began to decide what she would wear, what food she wanted to serve, and what her friends might like to do.

DRESSING UP

As soon as the friends arrived, they were whisked into Laura's room where, with much giggling, they donned their mother's old party dresses, applied makeup, and decked themselves with discarded costume jewelry. Laura offered to loan them sashes, bows, ropes of beads, and other accessories from her own costume box.

"How charming!" exclaimed Mr. Blake as the first of the ladies emerged from Laura's room into the living room. "May I please take your photograph?" Laura and her guests laughed as they watched

Mr. Blake imitate a portrait photographer. "Please lift your chin a little—so—place your hands—so—look this way. Smile a little, please. There, that's wonderful!" he was saying. Then to another guest, "May I also take your photograph?"

"Oh, yes!" said Laura, falling into her father's act. "We should each love to have a photograph taken by Blake Studios." Suddenly, she spied her mother who had, for a surprise, dressed up like a maid with a little white cap and apron. "Nannette," she said to her mother, "we should like to have luncheon served when Mr. Blake has finished taking pictures."

LUNCHEON

Although Laura enjoyed every minute of the play acting, she was practical enough to scurry into the kitchen and help her mother dish the food. It was simple, because chicken salad and nutbread sandwiches had been prepared in advance. Her mother made instant cocoa and cooked frozen green beans during the picture-taking period. Card tables had been set up before the party, with a lima-bean-lady place card at each place. Of course, each guest wanted to examine all the place cards before she took her own seat for luncheon. For dessert, Laura served petits fours which she had decorated.

STYLE SHOW

Equipment: fashion pictures for hostess, pencil and paper for each guest

"Ladies," said Laura, after the tables had been cleared. "I know that you are interested in the latest fashions. I also know that you are creative. I am going to describe some of the latest fashions and ask you to draw them." She gave each guest a piece of paper and a pencil. She then tried to imitate a commentator at a fashion show.

"As I describe a costume of high fashion, I shall ask you to draw it.

First, an afternoon creation with a low-down waist and air for flair." Laura had studied style magazines and picked out phrases. She had put them together into a fashion "lingo" and had practiced saying them. She sounded funny, but she didn't crack a smile as she pretended to be a fashion expert.

When sketches were completed, guests compared them. Then Laura exhibited the published picture. "Were you all drawing the same dress?" laughed Laura.

"You draw one, Laura. You're good at drawing," said her friend, Sally. "Let me be commentator." Sally picked up a magazine.

"Go ahead," said Laura. She hadn't planned on this turn of events, but it was fun. Everyone drew several costumes with one person and then another being commentator.

HUMBUG

Equipment: paper and pencil for each player; humbug block and chart for each table (block has these letters marked on its sides: B, H, A, E, M, L. Chart reads as follows: B = one body; H = one head; A = two antennae [feelers]; E = two eyes; M = mouth; L = six legs

"Ladies," said Laura, "we shall now play Humbug. The rules are as follows: Each person at a table has a turn to roll the block until someone rolls a B. She draws the body of a bug and the game starts. Each person rolls the block in turn. You must get a B to start. If you get a B, you may roll again. You must then get an H for the head. If you get an H, draw the head on the bug. Body must come first, and then head, in that order. After that, you may add any other part you need; antenna, eye, mouth, or leg. You continue to have a turn as long as you get a letter you need. When you fail to roll the letter you need, pass the block to the person next to you. The first person to complete a bug with one body, one head, two antennae, two eyes, one mouth, and six legs, calls, 'Humbug!' and wins the game."

"Ladies," said Laura, when guests had played all the Humbug

for which there was time, "you are all such wonderful artists that I want to give each of you a prize. The winners of Humbug may choose first." She presented them with a tray of dolls, dressed in crepe paper. Each doll had a ballpoint-pen body.

GENERAL SUGGESTIONS

This party is planned for any girl who likes to dress up and pretend that she is a lady. Many fourth graders can have as much fun making place cards, invitations, and favors as they will have at the party itself. A younger child can help make them and will delight in receiving them.

GAMES: If a hostess doesn't enjoy pretending that she is a fashion commentator, or thinks it is too hard for her, her mother or older sister may describe dresses. Guests may or may not take turns doing this, as they wish. Younger girls may draw a lady in a party dress, using their own imaginations completely.

You can play any table game you wish: GOING TO INDIA, PARCHEESI, LOTTO, or any of the simple games designed for children.

If you have six players or more, play at two or more tables so that no one has to wait a long time for a turn. You may give a prize for the table game if you wish; but it isn't necessary to do so. A lapel pin would be an appropriate prize.

LIMA-BEAN-LADY PLACE CARDS

Materials: dried lima beans; index cards or white cards, or stiff paper; colored pencils or paint; scraps of yarn; scraps of cloth; other decorations such as bits of feathers, veiling, beads, small artificial flowers, and so on; glue

Assemble material and equipment with which to work, including tweezers or a pin and sharp scissors. Lay a dried lima bean on the card and plan how to make a hat, collar, and front of a dress for a lady. Cut out little pieces of material and lay them in place. Draw a face on the bean. Make it simple. If you are using a colored pencil, moisten the tip so that the color will run onto the shiny bean.

Glue the lady's dress onto the card. If possible, use glue that comes in a tube and can be applied a drop at a time. Glue the bean face in place. Put glue around the edges of the bean and set bits of yarn in place for hair. Push it this way or that with tweezers or a pin. You may want to put on more than one layer of yarn.

Cut out material for a hat. Try it on the lady before you glue it in place. If you want the lady to have earrings, glue small beads in place. Do the same for a choker necklace or for a jewel in the lapel of her suit. You can glue a small piece of braid on her suit for trim. Glue a little flower on her hat, or a little feather. One small strand of a feather will suggest a long plume. Use your imagination as you design your ladies. Each lady should be different.

BUTTON-FACED-LADY INVITATION

Materials: button with two holes, paste or glue, yarn, colored pencil, crepe paper or cloth, narrow ribbon, blue construction paper

Cut a piece of blue construction paper 4 inches wide and 6 inches long. Lay a button on it and design a long dress for a lady with a button head. Cut out a piece of crepe paper a little longer than the skirt and a little wider than the width of the skirt. Put paste on the construction paper along the waist and the sides of the skirt. Gather the crepe paper along the top to fit the waist and along the edges. Leave the bottom unpasted. (The dress will look more finished if you turn under the side edges of the paper as you paste it in place.) Cut crepe paper the size and shape of the bodice of the dress. Paste it in place.

Draw a mouth on the button. The blue paper will show through the holes in the button for eyes. Paste the button in place on the shoulders of the lady. Glue yarn in place for hair. Cut a narrow ribbon and glue it onto the waist of the dress. Add a bow if you wish.

VARIATION. Instead of making a crepe paper dress, draw the picture of a lady with a button face.

LADY-PENCIL FAVOR

Materials: ball-point pen or pencil, crepe paper, pipestem cleaner, picture of lady's face, paste, empty spool, decorations if you wish

Don't spend too much time making this favor. The dress really serves as a wrapper for the gift.

Fold the top of the paper down 1 inch and pinch it together. Put the pen or pencil under the fold. Wrap a pipestem cleaner around the pencil near the top, letting the ends extend like arms of a doll.

Look in a mail-order catalogue or a magazine for the picture of a lady whose head is the right size for this doll—or draw a face. Cut out the picture. Paste it on top of the crepe paper. Insert the end of the pen or pencil into the center of an empty spool so that the lady will stand. If you wish, decorate the dress of the doll with stick-on stars, ribbon, or in any way you wish.

SPACE PARTY

A strange looking spaceman, with a tank attached to his back, arrived in the mail. Les Horvath soon discovered that the tank was really an invitation to Jim Harrison's Space Party (page 36). "Make a helmet for a man from space. Use a paper sack or box—not a plastic bag. Spacemen must breathe! Wear the helmet to the party," the instructions concluded.

"Mom! I need aluminum foil—to make a space helmet for Jim's party," Les called. "May I have some?"

"Help yourself," said his mother. "Do you need anything else?"

"Yes, lot's of junk," responded Les. Les was soon at work making his space helmet, and so were other boys and girls in the neighborhood.

SPACEMEN PARADE

A weird group of people entered the Harrison home on the day of the party, a group of spacemen, each wearing a space helmet decorated with "lots of junk"—spools, coat hangers, Tinker Toys, pipestem cleaners, and goodness knows what all.

"Let's have a parade of spacemen," said Jim when everyone had arrived.

"I think we should judge the helmets," suggested his mother. "This may be the first convention of spacemen. We ought to decide which helmets are best and why." She put slow music on the record player and encouraged the guests to walk in gruesome postures in time to the music.

AWARDS

Equipment: cellophane tape, ribbon award for each guest

"Stop!" said Jim's mother. "Stay where you are. I have judged your creations according to standards suitable to the space age. Jim, I appoint you Spaceman of the Day. Award the ribbons."

"Most fabulous helmet, Les Horvath," read Jim. Les received a ribbon, marked with his category. "Want to wear it on your helmet?" asked Jim.

"All right," agreed Les. Jim attached the ribbon to Les's helmet with cellophane tape.

Every spacemen received a ribbon. Some of the other categories were: most likely to stand sun rays; most antigravity; most absurd; most imaginative; most likely to go with the wind; most complicated.

PILOT AND COPILOT

Equipment: different colored construction paper circles cut in half

"Park your helmets around the room," Jim directed as the guests removed their headgear. "Before we go into space, we must have pilots and copilots. Close your eyes and draw a half-moon out of the box that I am going to pass around." In the box were different colored construction paper circles which had been cut in half. There was one half circle for each guest. "Match colors to find partners," Jim advised.

WORLDS IN COLLISION

Equipment: balloon and three-foot length of string for each pair of players

"Blow these balloons up so that they look like worlds," directed Jim. "Tie a string around each balloon." He gave a balloon and string to each pair of players. "Now, tie the loose end of the string around the

ankle of one of the partners. Partners stand side by side, with one arm around the other's waist. You must stay in this position or you'll be out of the game.

"The balloon is your world. You must protect it; and at the same time try to stamp on the other balloons and break them. If anyone breaks your balloon, you must drop out of the game."

What a scramble, and what a lot of noise! However, it didn't last long. Soon only one couple remained. "Here's to you on the Milky Way!" said Jim, as he handed each of the winning pair a candy bar.

KNOW THE PLANETS

Equipment for each couple: pencil and names of planets in mixed-up order

"I want to see if you know where you are going in space," said Jim. "Don't look at this until I tell you." He gave each couple a pencil and a list of the names of the planets with the letters mixed up.

The list read: thera, evsun, purijet, smra, remycur, tansur, tulpo, epunten, suruna. Jim knew that the list meant: Earth, Venus, Jupiter, Mars, Mercury, Saturn, Pluto, Neptune, Uranus. Jim didn't play this game because he was already familiar with the jumbled spelling.

First couple to write the correct names next to the mixed-up names won. They each received a candy bar. Other couples completed the list, sometimes with help.

BACK TO BACK

"You are doing very well together as pilots and copilots," remarked Jim's mother. "You defended your earth. You identified the planets. Now let's see what you can do when you are back to back."

Partners were asked to sit back to back with arms interlocked. At a signal, they tried to stand without unlocking arms. First couple up won candy bars.

FLYING SAUCER

Equipment: pie tin

"We'll practice catching flying saucers," Jim announced. Players sat in a circle. Jim gave each player, including himself, a number. Jim was IT. He turned the pie tin on its side on the floor, gave it a spin, and at the same time called a number, "Three."

THREE jumped up and caught the pie tin before it dropped to the ground. IT took THREE's place in the circle. THREE became IT and spun the platter. When a player failed to catch the platter, IT spun again. If two players in a row failed to catch the platter, IT chose another person to be IT.

WHAT DID A SPACEMAN LOOK LIKE?

Equipment: pencil and paper for each guest

The guests were still sitting in a circle. "Wonder what you saw in space," mused Jim. He gave each guest a pencil and a piece of paper. "Nobody knows what spacemen look like. We often draw them like boxes with antennae on their heads; but maybe they aren't like that at all. Maybe they look like animals, maybe snakes."

He asked each person to fold his paper in three parts and then draw the head of a spaceman on the top third, making little marks on the second section to show where the shoulders ended. Each person kept his drawing secret.

"Now, fold the paper so that the next person can't see the drawing,"

33

Jim instructed. "Pass the paper to the person at your right." The second person drew the body and arms of the spaceman, and made little marks where the legs should begin on the third section of the paper. He folded under his section and passed the paper to the third person who drew the legs and feet of the spaceman. Then everyone opened the paper he was holding. What sights!

TAKE ME TO YOUR LEADER

"When you meet spacemen, you'll want to meet their leader," said Jim. "We'll practice finding a leader."

The guests and Jim sat in a circle. Jim chose one to be ASTRONAUT. He left the room. Jim chose another player to be LEADER. LEADER selected a motion, such as patting his head. All the other players copied LEADER. ASTRONAUT was called back into the room. He stood in the center of the circle, turning around slowly, trying to find LEADER. LEADER changed his motion. All the other players copied LEADER. For example: When LEADER clapped his hands, they clapped their hands. When LEADER snapped his fingers, they snapped their fingers. LEADER tried to make these changes when ASTRONAUT's back was turned to him. LEADER made many changes. ASTRONAUT tried to guess quickly. If he guessed correctly, LEADER became ASTRONAUT. If after three guesses, ASTRONAUT could not identify LEADER, he asked, "Who is your leader?" Then he chose another ASTRONAUT, who left the room. Jim choose another LEADER.

REFRESHMENTS

"Time to return to earth," said Mother, as she invited the guests into the dining room. "Keep your helmets on, if you can eat. Otherwise, take them off."

At each place stood a gumdrop spaceman standing on a place card. "Better watch out when you eat him," warned Jim. "He's full of toothpicks."

"We won't eat that spaceman in the center," said Les, as he spotted the spaceman centerpiece (page 38) which Jim had constructed of boxes and this and that.

"This looks like the sun," remarked one of the little girls as she looked at the main luncheon dish. It was Holland rusk, topped with cheese rarebit. From it extended narrow strips of carrots, like rays of the sun.

"Sunlight orange juice to drink," remarked Mother. For dessert Jim served heavenly star-shaped cookies, which he had baked, and very earthly ice cream.

"Would you like to see how I made the spaceman?" asked Jim. He removed the top section of the centerpiece. The bottom section was filled with favors, one for each guest.

GENERAL SUGGESTIONS

This party is for children who like to make believe and who know their letters and numbers—children about six years old and older. It can be given indoors or outside.

GAMES: If you cannot play a noisy game where you live, omit WORLDS IN COLLISION and play HAIL ON THE HAT (page 119). Call it FALLING STARS ON THE EARTH.

If children are just learning to read, put signs around the room with the names of planets on them. As guests are working in pairs, they will be able to match the length of the words and write the correct words next to those on their papers.

If your guests are older, they may like to work on this game alone. You can make it more difficult by including the names of other heavenly bodies, such as constellations.

If the guests are five years old, omit this game.

If guests have trouble spinning the platter, substitute STAR NUMBER CHANGE (below).

FOOD. You could add IMP SALAD (page 149) to your menu. Call it SPACEMAN SALAD.

STAR NUMBER CHANGE

Players sit in a circle. Each is given a number. IT stands in the center of the circle. It calls two numbers: for example, STAR ONE—STAR SIX. Players with these numbers try to change seats. IT tries to slip into one of their seats. Player who is left standing in the center of the circle becomes IT.

INVITATION

Materials: construction paper, cellophane tape

Cut a piece of construction paper for a background. Make it small enough to go into the envelope you want to use. Draw a picture of a man from space with a tank on his back. Write the invitation on a narrow strip of paper. Roll it up like a tube. Use cellophane tape to fasten it onto the back of the figure. Write, "Look in my tank!" beneath the figure.

SPACEMEN'S HELMETS

Materials: boxes or paper bags, odds and ends

Boys and girls need little suggestion about how to make helmets for spacemen. They can make them out of paper bags and paint weird features on them. Or they can make them out of boxes covered with aluminum foil. Be sure to cut out eyes and nose and mouth in a helmet. *Do not use plastic bags!*

RIBBON AWARDS

Materials: blue construction paper, blue ribbon about ½ inch wide, crepe paper, paste, cellophane tape

Cut a circle, 2 inches in diameter, out of blue construction paper. Cut a strip of crepe paper, 1 inch wide, down 8 inches on the long side of a roll of crepe paper. Cut two pieces of blue ribbon 2 inches long.

Flute one edge of the strip of crepe paper to make it ruffled. Put paste around the edge of the circle. Paste the unruffled edge of the strip of crepe paper onto the back of the circle so that it makes a frame about ¾ inch wide. Cut off the extra end of crepe paper. Put a little paste on one end of each piece of ribbon. Paste the ribbons onto the back of the construction paper circle so that they hang down like ribbons won at a fair.

Print the category on the center of the award, such as "Most Fabulous," and so on. Have a category and an award for each guest. Always ask a winner if he would like to have the award attached to his helmet before you stick it on with cellophane tape.

VARIATION. You can make a simpler award without crepe paper. Cut a construction paper circle and construction paper "ribbons." Paste the ribbons onto the circle.

GUMDROP PLACE CARD

Materials: gumdrops, toothpicks, small card

Gumdrops come in all shapes, colors, and sizes. Fashion them into spacemen, holding the parts of the body together with toothpicks. Write the name of a guest on a small card. Stand the spaceman on the card.

SPACEMAN CENTERPIECE

Materials: one box for body, one box for head, wire, paints or aluminum foil, odds and ends, gifts to put in larger box

Choose a box with a lid for the body. Choose a smaller box for the head. Either paint the boxes with poster paint, or cover them with paper or aluminum foil. Be sure that you can remove the lid of the lower box. Make any kind of face you want and add arms, antennae, or anything that you think a man from space might have.

Put favors in the lower box. You may be able to find inexpensive gifts which your friends would like, such as small globes, or candy packaged in the shape of rockets, or little rocket guns. Or you can wrap packages of candy or gum so that they look like little rockets.

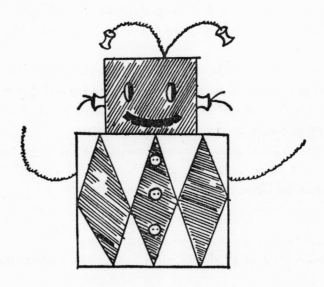

Valentine Party

"That's a new kind of valentine. Wonder why it came so early," said Terrie Powell, looking at a red heart with shutters (below). When she opened the shutters, she discovered that her valentine was

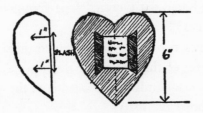

in reality an invitation to Jane Bryan's Valentine Party. The time, date of party, and Jane's address were written on paper behind the shutters.

KNAVE OF HEARTS

Equipment: chair, dish with candy hearts in it, paper crown

When everyone had arrived, Jane asked them to sit in a circle. "All our games today are going to be about the Queen of Hearts," she explained. "You all know the nursery rhyme—the Queen of Hearts baked some tarts and the Knave stole them." The guests nodded.

"These are tarts," continued Jane, picking up a bowl with candy hearts in it. "They aren't really tarts, but we'll pretend that they are." She placed the bowl of candy in the middle of the circle.

"This is the throne," she said. She placed a small chair near the candy. "Now, we need a Queen. We'll all say the nursery rhyme and I'll pick out a queen. Jane closed her eyes, stretched one arm out straight, and turned around and around as everyone recited:

> The Queen of Hearts,
> She made some tarts,
> All on a summer day.
> The Knave of Hearts,
> He stole the tarts,
> And then he ran away.

At the end of the verse, Jane opened her eyes. The person at whom she was pointing became QUEEN. Jane escorted her to the THRONE and placed the crown on her head. "Of course, if I had pointed to a boy, not a girl, he'd be King, not Queen," Jane commented. "Mother, will you explain the rules?"

These are the rules as Mrs. Bryan explained them: QUEEN sits on the THRONE in the center of the circle and shuts her eyes with her hands over them. The LEADER stands on the outside of the circle and points to someone who becomes the KNAVE.

KNAVE tiptoes toward QUEEN and tries to steal a piece of candy without her hearing him. If she thinks she heard him, she keeps her eyes shut, points in his direction, and calls, "Stop, thief!" Then she opens her eyes. If she is pointing in KNAVE's direction, he returns to his place in the circle. If she is pointing in the wrong direction, KNAVE takes her place on the THRONE and she takes his place in the circle. If KNAVE gets a piece of candy before QUEEN calls, he becomes KING.

If QUEEN stops three KNAVES before they can get candy, she chooses a new KING or QUEEN. Mrs. Bryan was LEADER. She crowned each new KING or QUEEN. At the end of the game, Jane passed around the bowl of candy, asking each guest to take one, two, or three pieces.

HEARTS DON'T FLY

"The poor Queen of Hearts!" sighed Jane. "She was so upset about her tarts! She began to think that they flew away. So people invented a game, HEARTS DON'T FLY. Mother, will you tell them about the game."

Mrs. Bryan asked everyone to stand facing her. Then she asked them to move their arms like flying birds. "Whenever I mention things that fly, move your arms like birds," she explained. "However, when I name something that does not fly, don't move your arms. Anyone who moves his arms at the wrong time is out of the game."

Mrs. Bryan started. "Robins fly. Bluebirds fly. Airplanes fly. Hearts fly." All who moved their arms on "hearts" dropped out of the game.

Mrs. Bryan continued, "Eagles fly. Trucks fly." The object of the game was to say the words clearly and quickly and to change the number of things mentioned, hoping that some players would keep on flying when they should stop. When only one person remained, he was proclaimed winner. As the guests were still interested in the game, the winner took Mrs. Bryan's place as LEADER.

THE QUEEN'S RINGS

Equipment: two rubber bands, string long enough to reach from player to player when they are sitting in a circle

"I guess that the Queen learned that some things fly and some things don't fly," said Jane. "Let's sit in a circle again." The guests did as directed. "The Queen had another problem," continued Jane. "with her rings. Long ago the Queen of Hearts gave two magic rings to her people. She said that as long as the people kept passing the rings from one person to another, the person who gave away a ring and the person who received a ring would have good luck. Now, there was a witch in the land. She didn't want the people to have good luck, so she tried to get the rings. This meant that the people had to pass them secretly, without letting the witch see them.

The player who had won the last game of HEARTS DON'T FLY became WITCH. She sat in the center of the circle. Jane took a piece of string, long enough to go around the circle, slipped two rubber bands over one end of the string, and tied the two ends of the string together to make a long loop. "These are the rings," said Jane, holding up the rubber bands. Jane gave the string to the players in the circle. She asked WITCH to close her eyes for a minute. Jane separated the RINGS so that they were on opposite sides of the circle. Players in the circle cupped both hands loosely over the string, making sure that the RINGS were hidden. WITCH opened her eyes.

The players who had the RINGS slid them along the string from player to player. The players who did not have a RING also slid their cupped hands back and forth over the string, pretending that they were passing the RINGS. WITCH tried to guess who had a RING.

When WITCH found a RING, the holder became WITCH. When by bad luck, a RING dangled from the string between two players, and the WITCH saw it, the player who had held the RING last became WITCH.

HUCKLE BUCKLE VALENTINE

Equipment: paper heart

"At last, the old witch gave up trying to get the rings," said Jane, as she took the string and rubber bands. "The Queen was very happy. In fact, she was so happy that she gave a Valentine's Day party to celebrate. Everybody played Huckle Buckle Valentine, just as we play Huckle Buckle Beanstalk."

"There are different ways to play Huckle Buckle Valentine," suggested Mrs. Bryan. "Let's use these rules today."

One player is IT. Everyone else leaves the room. IT quickly hides a paper heart some place in plain sight. The heart may be on a window sill, a radiator—any place where you can see it without moving anything. IT calls the other players to return. They hunt for the heart. The first player to see it says, "Huckle Buckle Valentine," and sits down. He may move away from the place where he has seen the heart, or he may sit close by. The hunt continues until everyone has seen the heart and is seated. The person who first found the heart may hide it for the next game.

EVERYONE A PRINCE OR PRINCESS

Materials: precut paper crown for each guest, decorations, paste, staples

"The Queen had such a good time at her party," said Jane, "that she decided to crown everyone a prince or princess. She had one problem—not enough crowns. So she asked everyone to make his own. We'll make ours, too."

Everyone helped to set up card tables. Jane gave each guest a pre-cut paper crown which had not been stapled into a circle. Mrs. Bryan put a supply of decorations in the center of each table. There were lace paper doilies which could be carefully torn apart, scraps of construction paper, gummed stars and other shapes—anything that could be cut into paper "jewels" and pasted onto a crown. When a guest had finished his crown, Mrs. Bryan fitted it to his head and stapled the ends in place. Then she crowned him "Prince Albert" or "Princess Terrie," or whatever his or her name was.

DANCING AT COURT

Equipment: music

"Your royal Majesties, let us have a court dance," suggested Mrs. Bryan. Everyone scurried to pick up scraps, fold card tables, and wash hands in preparation for a court ball.

Mrs. Bryan put some old love tunes on the phonograph and everyone danced. At last they went into the dining room for regal refreshments.

REGAL REFRESHMENTS

The table was centered with a valentine tree (page 46) and each place was marked with a valentine nut-cup place card. Jane served strawberry flavored fruit gelatine, crowned with whipped cream, heart-shaped sandwiches, heart decorated cake, and ice cream.

After lunch, she gave each guest a "make-your-own-valentine kit." "Only six days left until Valentine's Day," she reminded her guests as she bade them good-bye.

GENERAL SUGGESTIONS

This party is planned for children five years old, or older. You will have to decide whether the host or hostess is ready to tell the story about the Queen of Hearts. It may be well to have an adult direct all the activities, tying them together with a story. However, the hostess should understand the party plans, and should add information whenever she wishes. She can also help in many ways: with making the invitations, table decoration and crowns; passing out equipment, and so on.

HUCKLE BUCKLE VALENTINE. If it isn't convenient to send most of the guests out of the room, send two or three. In order to help the searchers find the heart quickly, other players call "hot" when anyone is near the heart and "cold" if everyone is far away. When a searcher finds the heart, he calls, "Huckle Buckle Valentine!" and sits down, as he did in the other version. When all the searchers have spotted the heart, each chooses a player to leave the room. The player who first found the heart may hide it for the next game.

HEARTS DON'T FLY. If the players are not yet ready for HEARTS DON'T FLY, substitute THE QUEEN SAYS "DO THIS" (below).

TABLE. If you do not care to make a valentine tree, center the table with the cake. Some party cookbooks have plans for making cakes that look like castles. Others have plans for making heart-shaped cakes.

THE QUEEN SAYS "DO THIS"

This game is like SIMON SAYS "DO THIS." One player stands in front of the group. He says, "The Queen says, 'Do this.'" He makes a motion. Other players make the same motion.

If IT says, "Do this" without mentioning the Queen, players must not make a motion. Anyone who makes a motion at the wrong time drops out of the game. IT should make motions quickly and catch as many players as he can. When only one player remains in the game, he becomes IT.

HEART INVITATION

Materials: red and white construction paper, paste

Cut out two hearts, one red and one white, at least 4 inches wide and 6 inches long. Fold the red heart in half the long way. Place your scissors on the fold a little below the dip in the top of the heart. Make a slash 1 inch wide. Two inches below this cut, make another slash 1 inch wide. Cut along the fold between the two slashes. Open the heart. Fold back the flaps, like shutters.

Paste the red heart on the white heart. Write the invitation on the open white space. Close the shutters. Make an envelope.

VALENTINE NUT-CUP PLACE CARD

Materials: one and a half pipestem cleaners; red, white, and yellow construction paper; cellophane tape; nut cup; crayons or pencils, paste

Cut a pipestem cleaner in half. Twist another pipestem cleaner around it to form arms for a valentine figure. Cut out a white heart for a face. Draw or color features on it. Cut out a crown and paste in place. Tape the face onto the top of the pipestem-cleaner arms.

Cut out a red heart for the body of the figure. It should be shorter than the half pipestem cleaner. Turn the heart point up. Write Queen or King and the name of a guest on this heart. Tape this onto the figure so that the point of the heart forms the neck of the figure. Reinforce the figure with more tape across the back of the half pipestem cleaner.

Make a slit near the rim of the nut cup. Make another slit ½ inch below it. Slip the part of the pipestem cleaner which extends below the heart into the two slots. Fasten in place with tape.

VALENTINE TREE

Materials: flowerpot, paper to cover it, stiff wire, pipestem cleaners, thread, three colors of construction paper

Invert the flowerpot. Twist several lengths of stiff wire together to form the trunk and main branches of the tree. Make smaller branches with the pipestem cleaners. Cover the flowerpot with paper.

Now make valentine blooms. Cut out three identical hearts from three shades of paper: for example, red, white, and yellow. (Valentines do not have to be red.) Fold each heart in half, the long way. Paste half of the red heart onto half of the white heart. Paste the other half of the white heart onto half of the yellow heart. Paste the remaining half of the yellow heart to the remaining half of the red heart. (You can make your heart-blooms all one color if you prefer.)

Thread a needle. Put it through the center of the heart-bloom. Fasten the thread to form a loop. Hang it on the tree. Make several heart-blooms.

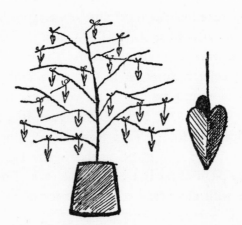

Several people can work on one heart tree; for example, members of a class, a Brownie Scout troop, Club Scout den, or members of a family.

St. Patrick's Day Party

"Do you have to be Irish to have a St. Patrick's Day Party?" Kathy Van Cleef asked her mother as they paused in front of a stationery store.

"Of course not!" laughed her mother. "But you'd better like green," she added pointing to the shamrocks, green pigs, leprechauns, and other Irish emblems in the store window.

"I could make invitations like that," mused Kathy. "It's just a leaf."

"Yes," agreed her mother, "a shamrock leaf, cut on a double sheet of paper. You could write the invitation on the inside sheet."

"Let's plan a St. Patrick's Day Party," said Kathy, "just for fun."

"Good idea," said her mother. During the raw windy days that followed, Kathy was very busy making invitations, decorations, and props for her party.

IRISH EYES TEAMS

"People talk about Irish eyes," said Kathy, when all her guests had arrived. "Let's see what color they are." She gave each guest a filing card with a big eye on it.

"My Irish eye is brown," said one guest.

"Mine is blue," said another.

"Oh, how lucky," said Kathy. "The blue Irish eyes will form one team and the brown Irish eyes will form the other team."

IRISH FROGS

Equipment: tablespoon and box for each team; potato for each player

"We all know that St. Patrick drove the snakes from Ireland, but the frogs stayed there," explained Kathy. "We know, too, that the Irish like potatoes. So we are going to have an Irish frog potato race."

Teams lined up with one player behind the other. Across the room, and in front of each team, Kathy placed a box containing a potato for each player. She gave a tablespoon to each leader and asked them to squat in froglike position.

At a signal, each leader hopped like a frog to the box in front of his team, spooned up a potato, and hopped back to his team. He was not allowed to touch the potato, and he had to hold the spoon with one hand. If he dropped the potato, he had to scoop it up without touching it and continue to race from the spot where the potato had rolled off the spoon.

When the leader returned to his team, he gave the spoon to the next in line who continued the race. First team to have everyone race like a frog won; but the game continued until everyone had had a turn to hop.

PASS THE POTATOES

Equipment: two boxes for each team; potato for each player

"Every Irish family loved potatoes," remarked Kathy. "It took family co-operation to get them from the potato patch to the table."

She asked the teams to get in line, side by side. She then placed a box containing a potato for each player in front of each leader and an empty box next to each end man. Teammates joined hands. The leader and the last man had one hand free. All the other hands had to remain clasped during the entire race.

At a signal, the leader picked up a potato with his free hand and transferred it to his other hand, which was clasped to his neighbor's hand. The potato was passed down the line in this manner. When the last man received it, he put it in a box, then raised his free arm and yelled, "Hurray for the Irish!" At this signal, his leader picked up another potato and started it down the line. At no time could the team break handclasps. If players dropped a potato, they had to bend down, without unclasping hands, and pick it up. This meant that the entire team had to bend a little. First team to get its potatoes in the second box won the race.

SHAMROCK RACE

Equipment: drinking straw for each player; paper shamrock for each team

"The Irish carried the shamrock wherever they went," said Kathy. "We'll do the same. However, we'll carry the shamrock by inhaling through a straw." She showed them how to put a paper shamrock at the end of a drinking straw, inhale through the straw, and hold the shamrock at the end of the straw.

Teams lined up with one player behind another for a relay race. Kathy gave each player a drinking straw and each captain a paper shamrock. At a signal, each leader picked up the shamrock by inhaling through the straw. He walked to the other side of the room and back to his team without touching his shamrock or letting it fall. He gave the shamrock to the next player in line, who repeated the action. The team to have each member walk with the shamrock and return won the race. Kathy added the scores for all the relay races and gave a package of lime drops to members of the winning team.

KISS THE BLARNEY STONE

Equipment: construction paper; for each player—paper circle, paper napkin or other blindfold

"They say that the Irish are great storytellers because they have kissed the Blarney stone," explained Kathy. "This is the Blarney stone," she continued, holding up a full sheet of construction paper, cut roughly to look like a stone. "You don't have to really kiss it—just kneel down, bend forward, and touch your head to the floor." She demonstrated.

Kathy placed the STONE on one side of the room and asked guests to go on the other side of the room. One by one, she blindfolded them, turned them around, and asked them to walk forward, kneel down, and pretend to kiss the STONE. No one was allowed to grope to find it—just kneel down and touch his head to the floor where he stopped. Kathy placed a small paper circle on the spot where each head had touched the floor. She gave a book of jokes to the player who came closest to the BLARNEY STONE.

EMERALD ISLE

Equipment: music, green sheet of paper for all but one player

"All the Irish love the Emerald Isle—that's what some people call Ireland," said Kathy. "We'll play Emerald Isle. It's something like Going to Jerusalem. Instead of chairs, we'll use islands," she added, holding up pieces of green paper.

Kathy placed the ISLES in a big circle and asked players to stand on the ISLES. Kathy joined the circle, making one more player than ISLE. Mrs. Van Cleef played the record player. Everyone marched around the circle, stepping on each ISLE as he walked. Suddenly the music stopped. The person not standing on an ISLE left the game, taking an ISLE with him. Each time that the music stopped a player withdrew. When only two players remained, Kathy presented each with an Irish favor.

PAT AND PATSY POTATO PUPPETS

"Where are Pat and Patsy?" asked Kathy.

"Right here," said Mrs. Van Cleef, holding up two potato puppets.

"They're cute!" said one guest.

"Let's make some and put on a show," said Mrs. Van Cleef.

Kathy gave each guest a potato with a round hole cut in the bottom while Mrs. Van Cleef put magic markers, crepe paper, cellophane tape, pins, and odds and ends on a card table. She gave each guest a piece of white cloth about the size of a man's handkerchief. "For clothes," she explained.

The guests constructed the puppets very quickly; and soon everyone was making his puppet dance up and down and sway back and forth in time to a tune which he hummed.

"Let's put on a show with lots of music," said Kathy.

"My puppet knows a riddle," said one of the boys.

"Let's hear it," said Kathy.

Goodness only knows how long the variety show might have lasted if Mrs. Van Cleef hadn't entered the room saying, "Faith and Be Gorra! Let's chase the snakes out of Ireland and then have supper."

"Chase the snakes?" said the guests.

SNAKE DANCE

"Yes," said Mrs. Van Cleef. "We'll have a snake dance and then eat. Bring your puppets if you like, and line up. Now put your left hand on the shoulder of the person in front of you." She turned on the record player and the guests wove in and out, like a long snake, around the room, and at last into the dining room.

REFRESHMENTS

In the center of the table was a big green hat (page 54), the kind that Paddy, himself, would have loved to wear on special occasions. A green ribbon extended to each place where there was a small green hat, set upside down. On the brim of each hat was written the name of a guest.

"Can I wear my hat? The candy inside is wrapped," said a guest.

"That's the idea," said Kathy, as she emptied her candy onto the

51

tablecloth and put her hat on her head at a jaunty angle. She slipped the elastic cord under her chin.

The guests were served hearty Irish food: scalloped potatoes, corn beef, green peas, and milk. For dessert they had shamrock-shaped cookies and big lime sodas (ice cream placed in tall glasses and lime soda poured over it).

After supper, everyone pulled the ribbon at his plate. The big center hat toppled over, and out came a small Irish favor for each guest.

GENERAL SUGGESTIONS

This party is planned for children seven years old and older. Five- and six-year-olds can also give the party if they know how to play relay games; or if you eliminate the relay games and substitute BLIND MIKE (below).

You can give this party in your home if you keep the guest lists small. Or your club or troop can give it in a social hall.

GAMES. If you have more than ten players, you will need more than two relay teams. To choose teams, pass out folded filing cards on which you have pasted Irish symbols, such as: harp, shamrock, green pig. Players with identical symbols form a team.

If players enjoy a certain relay game especially, repeat it.

If it isn't practical to play EMERALD ISLE because it is too noisy or because there isn't enough room, substitute BLIND MIKE (below).

FAVORS AND PRIZES. Ten-cent stores usually carry a wide variety of inexpensive St. Patrick's Day favors. You can choose pins or other small articles that children can wear. Or you can choose figurines. If the favors under the centerpiece hat are breakable, lift the hat and have the guests pull the ribbons gently. If you wish to add more table decorations, make pipestem-cleaner leprechauns with little green hats (page 61).

FOOD. Corn beef and the Irish seem to go together. However, if you wish, you can serve any other meat; for example, pressed canned meat, roast beef, or meat loaf.

BLIND MIKE AND HIS PIG

Equipment: men's handkerchiefs for blindfolds

Players form a circle. Two players stand in the middle of the circle and are blindfolded. One is PADDY PIG who gets down on all fours. The other is MIKE. MIKE calls, "Paddy Pig! Paddy Pig!" PADDY PIG must answer *"Oink, oink,"* each time his master calls.

PADDY and MIKE move around inside the circle. MIKE tries to catch PADDY. PADDY tries to keep away from MIKE. When MIKE touches PADDY, each chooses a new character.

SHAMROCK INVITATION

Materials: green construction paper

Cut a piece of green paper, 3 inches wide and 6 inches long. Fold it in half, making a 3-inch square. Draw a shamrock on the outer sheet, so that the top of the center leaf is on the fold. Write, "St. Patrick's Day Party" on the outer sheet. Write the date, time, place, and your name on the inside sheet.

POTATO PUPPET

Materials: medium-sized potato, piece of cloth the size of a man's handkerchief, magic marker, pins, construction paper, cellophane tape, odds and ends

Make a sample puppet before the party. Wash potato well and dry it. Carve a hole in the bottom of the potato, just large enough for your first finger. An apple corer is a good thing to use for this.

Draw features with a magic marker. Make a hat out of construction paper, crepe paper, and odds and ends. Use pins freely. You can stick them into the potato and not stick yourself when you play with the puppet.

For a costume, drape the piece of cloth over your hand. Hold up your first finger. Put the puppet on your finger.

Before the party, wash dry, and carve the center holes in the potatoes which the guests will use in making puppets.

PADDY'S HAT CENTERPIECE

Materials: large empty oatmeal box, construction paper, poster paint, paste

Remove the paper with printing on it from a large empty oatmeal box. Make the brim of the hat from green construction paper. Trace around the bottom of the box in the center of the paper. Draw a smaller circle, ½ inch inside this circle. Draw another circle with a radius 2 inches wider than the first circle. Cut out the biggest and the smallest circles.

Slash at ½ inch intervals from the center of the circle to the line. Turn these slashed pieces up. Paint the oatmeal box green. When the paint is dry, paste the brim of the hat onto the tall box. Make a paper hatband and bow and paste in place.

 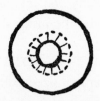

NUT-CUP HAT AND PLACE CARD

Materials: green paper drinking cup, construction paper, elastic cord 21 inches long

Place a paper drinking cup on a sheet of green construction paper and trace around it. Draw another circle with a radius 1 inch wider than this first circle. Draw a third circle with a radius ⅛ inch smaller than the circle that is the size of the cup. Cut out the largest and smallest circles.

Punch small holes on opposite sides of the drinking cup. Insert the ends of a 21-inch piece of elastic cord. Tie big knots on the ends. Put the cup on your head and pull the cord under your chin. Adjust the length of the cord if necessary.

Turn the cup upside down. Slip the hat-brim circle over the cup, gently pulling it down to the brim of the cup. Write the name of a guest on the brim of the hat. Place a few pieces of wrapped candy in the cup. The guest can empty the candy on the table, use the cup for a hat, then use it as a container to carry home his candy, if he hasn't eaten it all.

Toy Party

"Oh, look!" cried Sharon Vito, as she opened a letter addressed to her. "A teddy bear. His arms move. What does it say?"

"Phil Clark is having a Toy Party," explained her mother, reading the signs which the teddy bear held in his hands. "You are invited."

"What's a toy party?" asked Sharon.

"I really don't know," said her mother. "Wait and see."

When Sharon arrived at the Clark home, Mrs. Clark asked her if she would like to decorate a toy-soldier hat. Phil was busy coloring his. Sharon wanted to paste bright stars on hers. As more guests arrived, Phil and Sharon showed them how to decorate hats and helped them when they wanted help.

TOY SOLDIER PARADE

Equipment: music

"Let's have a parade of toy soldiers," suggested Mrs. Clark. "Put on your hats and get in line." She turned on the record player. Phil was the leader. He had practiced marching before the party. At first, not every child wanted to march; but before too long, everyone was going around the room, marching left, right, left, right.

FOLLOW THE LEADER

"Let's play follow the leader," said Mrs. Clark. "March as I do. Hands over head." She put her arms over her head and everyone else put his hands over his head. "Hands on your hips!" Again everyone copied her. "Lift your knees high." They were good toy soldiers and liked to obey commands.

ROLL BALL

Equipment: big ball

"Here is another toy," said Mrs. Clark.

"A ball," said Phil.

"Yes," said Mrs. Clark. "Sit in a circle. Put your legs far apart." They did as she directed. "Now, I'll roll the ball to Phil." Phil caught the ball and said, "I'll roll the ball to Sharon." Sharon rolled the ball to Tommy. Tommy didn't want to say anything, but he looked at Phil and rolled the ball to him. Back and forth across the circle the ball went.

PIN THE BOW ON THE TEDDY BEAR

Equipment: large picture of teddy bear on bulletin board; blindfold, paper bow, and thumbtack for each guest

"What's this?" asked Mrs. Clark as she held up a big picture which was thumbtacked to a bulletin board.

"A teddy bear," everyone answered.

Mrs. Clark propped the picture against one wall where all could see it. "This teddy bear would like a bow tie. I am going to give Phil a bow tie, and he'll put a thumbtack in it." Phil took the bow tie. "Now, I'll blindfold Phil and turn him around three times." She did so. "Now, Phil, walk up to the teddy bear and put the bow tie where it belongs." Phil pinned the big paper bow on the teddy bear's toe.

"I want to do it," said Sharon. She put the bow on the teddy's tummy. Everyone tried the game, although one guest didn't want to be blindfolded. He closed his eyes tight and pinned the bow on the teddy's ear. The children laughed to see the funny, funny teddy bear, with bows all over him—except at his neck where a bow should be. There was no prize.

TOY PICTURES

Equipment: pictures of toys, including jack-in-the-box
"Here are the other toys," said Mrs. Clark. "Tell me what they are." She held up one picture and then another as the children called out the names of the toys. The last picture was a jack-in-the-box.

JACK-IN-THE-BOX

"Do as I do and say the little verse after me," said Mrs. Clark.
"This is Jack (*Clench left fist with thumb extended.*)
In a box. (*Put thumb in left fist. Cover with palm of right hand.*)
Open the lid. (*Lift right hand.*)
Out Jack pops!" (*Pull thumb out of fist with a jerk.*)
The guests played JACK-IN-THE-BOX several times.

REFRESHMENTS

"Time for toys to march again," said Mrs. Clark. "I'll just say, 'Left, right.'" The guests formed a line and followed Phil and his mother into the dining room.
Everyone was seated. At each place was a pipestem-cleaner doll.

"She can go in my doll house," said Sharon.

"He can ride in my truck," said Phil.

In the center of the table was a long, low box marked TOY BOX. From it extended streamers leading to each place. Some of Phil's toys, all scrubbed and dried for the big day, clambered over the centerpiece box.

In front of each guest was a plate of small sandwiches, each wrapped in wax paper. Mrs. Clark also served carrot strips, milk, gelatin dessert, and cookies cut in the shapes of toys.

GENERAL SUGGESTIONS

This party is planned for children three, four, or five years old. Keep the guest list small. If the host is five years old, you may want to add a game from CIRCUS PARTY (page 98), or let the children draw or color pictures of toys.

Although it may be easier for you to do everything yourself, plan to let the young host help you whenever possible. He can help make the invitations and put them into envelopes for mailing, drop them into the mailbox, press the folds in the paper hats, roll dough and cut out cookies, put paper plates and napkins on the table, and greet guests at the door.

Most children three years old and over love a small party. However, they may hesitate to join activities that are new to them. Be patient. Encourage every child to do what others are doing; but don't force him to do it. Encourage the host to "play party" in advance. March in time to music and play the party games. A host likes to be a leader. However, save some surprises for him.

As a rule, there is one young guest who just loves to do anything suggested. Her enthusiasm is usually contagious. Keep the party relaxed. If the guests want to play informally with toys you have on hand instead of doing the activities you have planned, let them do so.

Remember that, as a rule, a three-year-old doesn't stay with one activity very long.

It is a good idea to have two older people at a preschool party: two mothers, or a mother and an older child. Don't leave children alone, without an older person with them. If you do not have someone to help you, serve refreshments which you can put on the table in advance.

Food. You can buy cookies shaped like toys. Or you can bake your own, using cutters shaped like animals, dolls, rocking horses, etc.

INVITATION

Materials: construction paper, paste, two-prong paper fasteners

Draw the pattern of a teddy bear with arms separate from the body. Cut out the pattern. Mark on the body where the arms should be fastened. Mark on the arms where fasteners should be inserted. Trace the pattern onto paper and cut it out. Hold a punch over the dots which mark the positions for joining arms and body. Encourage the host to punch the holes. (Using a punch helps to strengthen the small muscles of his hands.) Fasten the arms and body together with two-prong paper clips. Encourage the child to spread the prongs. Write the invitation on two small pieces of paper. Paste one on each paw of the teddy bear.

TOY SOLDIER HAT

Materials: shelving paper, staples, crayons, paste-on stars

Cut a piece of shelving paper 20 inches long. Fold it in half the long way. Place it on a table with the open edges toward you. Mark the center on the fold. Fold the upper-left-hand corner down from this center mark. Press the fold with the hands.

Fold the upper right-hand corner down from the center mark. Press the fold. Fold the dangling edges up on each side of the hat to make a brim. Staple this brim in place. Guests can decorate hat at party.

PIN THE BOW ON THE TEDDY BEAR

Materials: paper, crayons or paint or magic marker; bulletin board or heavy cardboard, thumbtacks

This game is like the traditional PIN THE TAIL ON THE DONKEY which you can use if you do not care to make your own game. You will have to determine the best way for you to hang up or prop up the game and the best way to pin the extra pieces on the main picture. Do not put pins or thumbtacks into wallpaper, plaster, wallboard, or wood paneling.

To make your own game, draw a large picture of a teddy bear. Thumbtack it onto a bulletin board. Cut out a paper bow tie for each guest. Put a thumbtack into the bow as you hand it to each player.

If you do not have a bulletin board, mount the picture on heavy cardboard or on the side of a large cardboard carton.

TOY BOX CENTERPIECE

Materials: cardboard box, shelving paper, pictures of toys, crayons or magic marker, paste, ribbon for each guest

Cut away most of the sides of a cardboard box, leaving the corners as they are. Cover the box, including the sides, with shelving paper. Write TOY BOX on each side. Paste pictures of toys on the box.

Choose small toys as gifts. Inexpensive plastic jack-in-the-boxes would be perfect for this party. Tie a ribbon to each gift. Place gifts under box. Extend a ribbon to each place.

PIPESTEM-CLEANER DOLL

Materials: one and a half pipestem cleaners, small piece of cloth or crepe paper

Fold a pipestem cleaner in half. A loop at the top forms the head of the doll. Twist the two ends of the cleaner around each other three times, ½ inch from the bend.

This twisted part is the body. Separate the two ends for legs. Turn up the last ¼ inch for toes. Take half of another pipestem cleaner. Twist it once, at the center, around the doll's body. The ends are the doll's arms.

Twist cloth or crepe paper around the doll for clothes. Bend the legs, so that the doll can sit down.

PLACE CARDS. Children who cannot read care little about place cards. However, if you want guests to sit in specific places, write their names on white cards. Set a pipestem cleaner doll on top of each card.

SAFARI PARTY

The word SAFARI was written in big purple letters across the front of the party invitation which Clyde Armstrong sent to his frends. On the inside sheet of paper were written the date, time, and place of the party and instructions to wear slacks or other play clothes.

JUNGLE SURVEY

Equipment: for each guest—filing card, pencil, pin, name of a big animal written on paper

"When my Uncle Ben went on a safari, he wasn't sure what animals he would see," Clyde told his guests when all had arrived. "We'll start the party with a jungle survey." He gave each guest a pencil and paper. Then he pinned the name of a jungle animal on the back of each guest. "Don't let anyone see this," Clyde warned. "No fair peeking until the game starts.

"These are the rules," Clyde explained. "Try to keep people from reading your card. You are not allowed to stand with your back against something, such as a wall. However, you may wiggle so that no one can read the card.

"Try to read other cards. When you see a name, write it down. First person to get all the names wins."

"Every game that we play today will start with a whistle," added Mrs. Armstrong. She pinned a name on Clyde's back. He didn't enter the contest because he had seen all the names. But he tried to keep other players from reading his.

After ten minutes of play, Mrs. Armstrong blew the whistle, and the hunt stopped. Clyde awarded a candy-bar tiger (page 68) to the winner.

PEANUT HUNT

Equipment: small sack for each player, peanuts—some painted different colors hidden around room or play area

"Uncle Ben said that they needed lots of peanuts to feed elephants on a safari," said Clyde. "See how many each of you can find." He gave each guest a small sack.

"Hey! I found a black peanut," yelled Joe.

"I found a red peanut," called Anne.

"Keep them," said Clyde.

When everyone had found all the peanuts he could, Clyde blew a whistle. "Sit in a circle," he directed. "Now count your peanuts." The person who had the most peanuts won a jungle lollipop. There were other prizes, too: a jungle lollipop for each colored peanut.

"I didn't know that they were special," said Gene.

"Lots of surprises on a safari," commented Mrs. Armstrong.

COUNT OFF FOR RELAYS

"Uncle Ben said that the safari group always formed parties," explained Mrs. Armstrong. "Stay seated and count off." The players counted, "One, two, one, two—" around the circle. Number ones formed the first team and number twos formed the second team.

PEANUT PASS

Equipment: spoon for each player; for each team—equal number of peanuts in a bowl and an empty bowl

"Uncle Ben said that everyone had to help feed the elephants on a safari," said Clyde. "We'll see how well you can co-operate." Clyde gave each player a teaspoon.

Players lined up side by side. Clyde placed a bowl of peanuts at the head of each line and an empty bowl at the end of each line. The players passed the peanuts at follows: At the sound of the whistle, each leader scooped up a peanut from the bowl. Teammates then passed the peanut down the line from spoon to spoon. No one was allowed to touch a peanut. If a peanut was dropped, the player who was passing it had to scoop it up with his spoon, without touching it with his hands, return to his place in line, and pass it to the player next to him. When the peanut reached the end of the line, the end player dropped it into the empty bowl. He then came to the head of the line, scooped up a peanut and passed it as before. At least the original leader was at the end of the line. As he dropped his peanut into the bowl, he yelled, "Hold it!" First team to have its leader yell, "Hold it!" won. The group played this relay three times.

CROCODILE RACE

"Uncle Ben said that his party had trouble with crocodiles," said Mrs. Armstrong. "We'll have a crocodile race." The guests practiced the crocodile run in this position: Squat. Place hands behind you on the ground. Lift hips off ground, supporting body with hands and feet.

Walk as fast as you can. Of course, you'll travel headfirst which makes you look as if you are going backward."

As the whistle blew, teams lined up on one side of the room with one teammate behind another. The whistle blew again. Each leader got into the crocodile position, raced to the opposite side of the room and back again. He touched the next player in line who ran the same way. First team to have everyone run the crocodile race won. However, the race continued until everyone had had a turn. Running this race once was enough.

BUILDING TRAPS

Equipment: fifteen toothpicks for each player; pop bottle for each team

"Uncle Ben said that building traps for animals took skill and patience," Clyde explained. "To make a trap, men dug a hole and covered it with little sticks. When an animal stepped on the sticks, it fell into the pit. We are going to try to pile up little sticks."

Mrs. Armstrong asked each team to sit in a circle. She put a pile of toothpicks in the center of each circle. "I'd like you each to count out fifteen toothpicks," she said. She also put a pop bottle in the center of each group.

"These toothpicks are sticks," said Clyde. The guests built the trap as follows: One player gently laid a toothpick across the opening of the popbottle. The next player did the same. If toothpicks fell as a player was adding his to the stack, he had to add all that dropped to his collection. The game continued with each player in each circle taking his turn. At last one player placed his last toothpick on the pile without causing any to fall. He was the winner. However, each team counted all the toothpicks resting on its bottle at the end of the contest. The team with the most won.

IN AND OUT OF THE NET

Equipment: ball of cord for each team

"Uncle Ben said that sometimes hunters got themselves entangled in nets," said Clyde. "Of course they had to get out," he added. The next relay was IN AND OUT OF THE NET.

Teams lined up with players standing side by side. Mrs. Armstrong gave each leader a ball of cord. The leader held the end of the cord in one hand and the ball in the other. At the sound of the whistle, the leader passed the ball around his body, winding himself with the string, and passed the ball to the next in line who did the same thing. When the endman had wound himself, he began to unwind, rewinding the cord on the ball as he did so. The ball was then passed down the line as each player untangled himself. When the leader held the re-wound ball in his hand, he yelled, "Free!" The team whose leader first yelled "Free" won the race. The guests wanted to try this relay race again.

Mrs. Armstrong quickly tallied the results of all the relays. The team with the most points was judged the best safari team and given first choice of jungle lollipops.

JUNGLE SOUNDS

"Uncle Ben always said that night was eerie in the jungle," said Mrs. Armstrong. Count off in threes and I'll let you find out what it sounded like." The players sat in a circle and counted off, "One two, three."

NUMBER ONES were asked to say in a very high voice, "High tomato, high tomato, high tomato."

NUMBER TWOS were asked to say in a medium voice, "Medium tomato, medium tomato, medium tomato."

NUMBER THREES were asked to say in a very low voice, "Fried bacon, fried bacon, fried bacon." Each group practiced its sound, one group at a time. Then when the whistle blew, all began to call at once. It did sound like a jungle frog pond. Mrs. Armstrong blew her whistle to stop the noise.

JUNGLE ANIMALS

Materials: peanuts, small potatoes, pipestem cleaners, extra-heavy toothpicks, buttons, odds and ends, glue

"Great Uncle Ben didn't see all the animals in the jungle, did he, Mom?" asked Clyde.

"Gracious, no!" said Mrs. Armstrong.

"Let's make some models of our own," suggested Clyde. Everyone helped to set up card tables with four people at a table. In the center of each table, Clyde and his mother placed a small plastic tube of glue, a quantity of peanuts, some small potatoes, pipestem cleaners, extra heavy toothpicks and odds and ends. The guests began by placing objects together to see if they looked like anything, and then began fastening the parts together with toothpicks. They added horns, and eyes, and tails—whatever the animal needed. Mrs. Armstrong excused herself and went into the kitchen while the guests created animals.

Mrs. Armstrong returned to view the weird creatures. "Let's have a jungle parade," she suggested. Guests placed the jungle creatures on the mantle and then helped to remove the extra materials and equipment from the card tables. Clyde gave each guest a napkin and a jungle placemat which he set on one of the card tables.

REFRESHMENTS

"Are we going to have a jungle menu?" asked Clyde.

"No," said Mrs. Armstrong, "Uncle Ben couldn't bring home any lion steak or elephant steak. But he did stop at the Galapagos Islands where they have big turtles. Clyde, will you please help me serve?"

"Turtleburgers!" cried the guests as they looked at the first plate. They also had Witch Doctor's brew (grape juice) which Clyde said that his Great Uncle Ben had learned to make in Africa, sugar cookies cut in animal shapes and monkey-see-monkey-do ice-cream bars—exactly the kind that Clyde bought whenever he had a chance.

FAVORS

"Did your Great Uncle Ben really go on a safari," asked Joe.

"No," said Clyde, "That's just a story." Stories reminded Clyde that he had a favor for each guest—an inexpensive book about animals.

GENERAL SUGGESTIONS

This party is planned for boys and girls, seven years of age and older. It can be given outdoors or in a home.

GAME. *Survey.* If guests cannot read, pin pictures on the backs of the guests. When a guest sees a picture, he runs to the adult leader and tells her the name of the animal. She writes the name on the player's card.

Relays. Relay games require careful supervision. An older boy or girl who is accustomed to directing games, or an adult, should be in charge.

An older host can assume more responsibility than a younger one.

Limit the number of players on a team to four or five. You can have three players on a team if the party is small. As a rule, the host likes to enter a contest.

Don't ask girls wearing skirts to run the crocodile race. Substitute GIANT FROG RELAY (below).

Extra game. If you need another game, play MUMBO JUMBO (below).

MAKING ANIMALS. You can use vegetables other than potatoes; for example corn cobs, peanuts, or summer squash.

GIANT FROG RELAY

The runner takes the following position and hops like a frog: Squat. Clasp hands in front of knees. Hop to goal and back without unfolding hands. Run race relay fashion with teams in line.

MUMBO JUMBO

One player is WITCH DOCTOR. Other players take partners and stand in a circle. WITCH DOCTOR gives a direction such as, "Back to back." Players do as directed. "Side to side." "Face to face."

Suddenly WITCH DOCTOR calls, "Mumbo Jumbo!" WITCH DOCTOR dashes to get a partner. All other players must take new partners. Player left without a partner becomes WITCH DOCTOR.

TIGER CANDY FAVOR

Materials: candy bar in yellow wrapping, paper, crayons, glue, pipestem cleaners

Use either a candy bar wrapped in yellow paper, or wrap a candy bar in yellow crepe paper. Draw and color the face of a tiger. Cut it out. Glue it onto one end of a candy bar. Insert pipestem cleaners for legs and tail. Don't spend too much time on candy favors as they are quickly pulled apart.

ANIMAL LOLLIPOPS

Materials: large flat lollipops, glue, paper, crayons

Draw heads of animals and color them. Cut them out. Glue them onto one side of lollipops.

PALM-TREE PLACE MAT

Materials: paper toweling, construction paper, paste

Tear off a section of a roll of paper toweling for a place mat. Design a simple palm tree with trunk and separate leaves that will fit onto the place mat. Using this as a pattern, cut trunks from brown construction paper and fronds from green. You can cut several trunks or fronds at a time. Paste tree on place mat. Keep these simple. They are attractive; but chances are that they will be used only once.

TURTLEBURGER

Materials: hamburger rolls, hamburgers, carrot strips, small sweet pickles

You can place the hamburger rolls, carrot strips, and pickles in place on paper plates before the party. Fry the hamburgers. Place them in a covered dish or wrap them in foil and keep them in the oven set on "warm." Place the fried hamburger on the roll when it is time to serve refreshments.

The body of the turtle is a hamburger roll. Slivers of raw carrot form his legs, tail, and neck. His head is a little pickle.

TRAVEL PARTY

"Look!" said Ingrid Jensen, as she opened the envelope addressed to her. "A passport!"

"A passport?" questioned her mother as she looked at the card. "Oh, a passport to Brenda's Toth's Travel Party." They talked about passports. Then Ingrid called Brenda to tell her that she had always wanted to travel and would love to come to her party.

TRAVEL TEAMS

Equipment: cards with pictures of steamships and airplanes

"Hello," said Brenda as she greeted each guest. "Here's your reservation. Hang onto it." Brenda gave each guest a card. Half the cards had pictures of airplanes on them and the other half had pictures of steamships.

SUITCASE RELAY

Equipment: for each team—suitcase containing hat, woman's skirt, man's jacket, pair of work gloves, shoes, and short-handled umbrella

"Before you go anywhere, you'll have to pack your suitcases," said Brenda. "We'll start the party with a suitcase relay." The players holding airplane pictures formed one team and the players holding steamship pictures formed the other. They lined up in relay fashion, one player behind the other. Brenda gave each leader a suitcase containing a hat, a woman's skirt, a man's jacket, a pair of work gloves, a pair of men's shoes, and a short-handled umbrella.

At a signal, each leader ran to the opposite wall, opened the suitcase, put on hat, skirt, jacket, gloves, and shoes; opened the umbrella; and closed the suitcase. She did not have to button or zip the jacket. She held the suitcase in one hand and the umbrella in the other and somehow managed to hold up the large skirt as she "slushed" back to her team as fast as she could without stepping out of her big shoes. She then closed the umbrella, and took off the hat, shoes, skirt, jacket and gloves, put them in the suitcase, closed the suitcase, and gave it to the next player in your line who repeated the action.

First team to have each member run, dress and return, won the race; but everyone had a chance to pack for the trip. Members of the winning team received chewing gum—to settle their stomachs on the trip ahead, Brenda explained.

DROP THE HANDKERCHIEF

Equipment: handkerchief

"First country we'll visit is Japan," said Brenda. "You may be surprised to learn what game children play there. Drop the handkerchief! They play it just as we play it.

"You may be IT," said Brenda, handing the handkerchief to one of the guests. "Let's make a circle." IT ran around the outside of the circle and dropped the handkerchief behind Ingrid. As soon as Ingrid saw the handkerchief behind her, she picked it up and chased IT around the circle, trying to catch her before she could get into the vacant space. IT reached the vacant spot safely, so Ingrid became IT. Whenever IT was caught, she remained IT and dropped the handkerchief a second time. But if she was caught a second time, she chose someone to take her place.

MORRA

"I'm tired of running. Let's sit down on our way to Italy," said Brenda. "We'll play a game Italian children play called Morra. When the leader calls 'Morra,' everyone puts out his right hand with a certain number of fingers extended. Like this—"

She held out her right hand with three fingers up, and thumb and little finger down. "You can have any number up. Thumb counts as a finger. As you put out your hand, call a number. Then we'll count the fingers that are up and the person who comes closest to that number wins the round and may call 'Morra' next time."

71

The children played the game for a few minutes. It was confusing to have so many people calling at once; but it gave them a chance to let off steam without too much exercise.

"It's a good game for three people as well as a party game," explained Brenda.

MOVING DAY

Equipment: folded newspaper for each pair of players

"We are going north to Denmark," said Brenda. "The children there play a game that is something like several games we play, including Fruit Basket Upset.

"This game is called Moving Day. Each of these papers represents a house. Every couple wants to live in a house. We'll put the houses in a big circle." The guests helped her put the papers in a circle. "This paper is a hotel," continued Brenda. She put it in the center of the circle. "No one wants to live in the hotel."

Players counted off for partners. One couple stood on the HOTEL, the center newspaper. Other couples stood on the HOUSES, the newspapers in the circle. When the couple in the center called, "Moving Day," every couple rushed to get a new HOUSE. The couple in the center also rushed to get a HOUSE. The couple left without a HOUSE moved into the HOTEL until they called, "Moving Day!"

SHOPPING

"Of course, we'll want to shop when we visit new cities," said Brenda. "Let's sit down and think about it." The guests sat in a circle with Brenda in the center. She explained the game. IT stood in the center of the circle and said, "In London (naming any city), I bought L—(the first letter of the city named), pointed to someone, and counted to ten. Before the count of ten was reached, the player at whom she was pointing had to name some object starting with the letter "l" that a person might buy. The player might say, "lamp," or "lace," or "lamb."

If he named an object correctly and in time, IT tried to catch someone else. If he did not name an object correctly or before the count of ten, he became IT. No one could repeat the name of a city or object.

REFRESHMENTS

Ladies and gentlemen, will you join us for supper?" asked Brenda's mother. The guests gladly accepted the invitation.

In the center of the table was a little train pulling boxcars (page 75), loaded with tiny wrapped gifts. Ribbon streamers led from the gifts to each place. At each place was an apple, round as the world, with a foreign flag on a toothpick standard stuck into the top. There were no placecards. "Sit where you wish," said Brenda.

The guests were served Italian spaghetti, lettuce wedges, big round oatmeal cookies, and of course, the apples. After dinner, Brenda suggested that each one follow the ribbon from his place to the box car and gently lift out the favor. Each guest received a small gift stamped with the name of a foreign country.

GENERAL SUGGESTIONS

This party is planned for a group of at least eight boys or girls six years of age and older. Unless you make changes, the party should be held out-of-doors, in a recreation room, or a social hall or gym where players can do a certain amount of running.

GAMES. *Relay race.* You can have more than two teams for relay races. Use pictures of trains or cars if you have enough players for three or four teams. You should have at least four people on a team. The host may run if an adult is directing the relay.

Shopping. If the guests do not know the names of many cities, IT may say, "When I was traveling, I bought B—" (or any letter) and count to ten. The person at whom he is pointing must name something that starts with B before IT reaches the count of ten. No name of an object may be repeated.

73

If the guests have not had experience with letters, play the game with categories: toys, clothing, food. IT says, "When I was traveling, I bought a toy" and counts to ten. The one at whom he is pointing must name a toy before the count of ten is reached. No object may be repeated.

If the guests are too young to play this game, substitute some well-known English game, such as: LONDON BRIDGE, HERE WE GO ROUND THE MULBERRY BUSH, MARCHING ROUND THE VILLAGE.

Moving Day. If you have fewer than ten players, don't play MOVING DAY with couples. All but one player sits on a chair, which is a HOUSE. It stands in the center, the HOTEL. When IT calls "Moving Day," everyone tries to get a different chair and IT also dashes for a chair. The player left standing is IT.

Morra. If you have a large number of guests, more than eight, play MORRA with each team forming a circle.

Quiet games. If you cannot play running games, play WHAT'S MISSING? (page 115), calling it WHAT DID I LOSE? or WHAT DID YOU SEE? (below). If you have additional time, play GUESS WHAT I BOUGHT (below).

WHAT DID YOU SEE?

Equipment: large sheet of paper, twenty-five pictures, paste; paper and pencil for each player

Paste on a large sheet of paper twenty-five pictures of things that you might see in a foreign country, such as: mountains, tree, man, and so on. Let guests look at pictures for five minutes. Remove poster. Ask guests to list all things they can remember.

GUESS WHAT I BOUGHT

One player pantomimes what he bought. She may try on a hat, bounce a ball, rock a doll, or do something harder to guess such as playing castanets. First person to name the purchase correctly, has a turn to pantomime what he bought.

VARIATION. Divide into teams. One member from each team comes to a table where you show them a picture of some object that might be purchased. Players return to teams and pantomime until a team member guesses the object. No one may make a sound while pantomiming. First team to guess correctly wins a point.

Different representatives then come forward and look at a new picture.

FLAG

Materials: paper, paints or crayons, glue, sturdy toothpick

You can buy inexpensive foreign flags, about 2 inches wide, at many variety stores. If you cannot buy them, copy pictures of flags from a dictionary or from an encyclopedia. Choose flags that are easiest to draw. Cut the flag about ½ inch wider than you want it to be when finished. Glue one side of the flag to a sturdy toothpick, winding it around the toothpick a little.

TRAIN CENTERPIECE

Materials: empty round salt carton; two cardboard processed cheese cartons; button; two empty spools; double-prong paper fasteners; glue; milk-bottle tops; pipestem cleaners; poster paints or latex paints; light-weight cardboard, such as suit box (See VARIATION, below)

You can use a toy train with open freight cars as a centerpiece, or you can make an old-fashioned train centerpiece. You can use it later to hold Christmas cards.

ENGINE. The tank of the engine is an empty salt carton. The cab and the base of the engine are the covers of two cardboard cartons in which processed cheese comes. The coal car and freight cars are the bottoms of the cheese cartons.

Cut 1½ inches from the bottom of the sides and ends of one cheese-box cover. This leaves a shallow box about 1 inch high.

Remove the outside paper from the salt carton. Take off the lid. Set the salt carton on its side and fasten it onto the shallow cheese-box lid with two-prong paper fasteners so that the end of the box and the end of the round carton are flush. Glue cover back on the salt box.

Hold the cheese-box cover in place so that it looks like the cab of an engine. Cut about 3½ inches from the end of this cover. Glue the back of the engine cab onto the end of the engine. The cab should be open in the rear.

To make a smoke stack, cut a half circle of light-weight cardboard 4 inches in diameter. Roll it into a funnel. Glue the overlapping edge in place. Make a hole in the top of the engine. Insert the smoke stack. Glue the empty spools in place for sand dump and whistle.

If you want to add a cowcatcher, cut a piece of light-weight cardboard 22 inches long and 2 inches wide. Fold it in half to make a piece 11 inches long and 2 inches wide. Rub the crease to make it sharp. Glue the strip onto the sides of the box so that the point sticks out in front of the engine.

CARS. Use the bottom of the cheese cartons for the coal car and the open freight car.

Paint the engine and the cars with poster paint or latex paint. If you find that poster paint will not cover the writing on the cheese cartons, add one tablespoon of soap flakes—not detergent—to one half cup of poster paint. As you paint the engine, be sure to paint a window frame and leave an unpainted window in the cab so that the engineer can look out ahead. Paint milk-bottle tops for wheels.

When the paint is dry, fasten the milk-bottle-top wheels in place on the engine and the cars with two-prong paper fasteners. Glue a button in place on the front of the engine for a headlight. Fasten the engine and the cars together with pipestem cleaners. If you want trim, attach decorative gummed tape.

VARIATION. You can use any combination of empty round carton (such as a small oatmeal carton or cornmeal carton) for the engine and oblong cartons (such as milk cartons or orange juice cartons) for the cab and cars. You can use a carton with a pointed top for the cab and flat-topped cartons for cars.

SPRING PARTY

"Judy had a party. I want to have a party," said Debbie Snyder.

"A good idea," said her mother. "What kind of party?"

"A party like Judy's," said Debbie.

"Oh, no! Not like Judy's!" laughed Mrs. Snyder. "Judy had a slumber party for eighth-grade girls."

"It's spring," suggested Judy. "How about a spring party, Debbie? We could make wheelbarrows to carry invitations. You could help make them."

Debby, Judy, and their mother talked about whom they should invite to the party and then made wheelbarrow invitations (below). They also made a paper basket for each guest. Each basket was a different color (page 86). They also cut out many flowers, the same colors as the baskets. On the day of the party, Debbie, Judy, and Mrs. Snyder placed the flowers around the living room.

"They look like a little garden," said Judy.

"They are easy to find," said Debbie.

FIND SPRING FLOWERS

Equipment: a paper basket for each guest, flowers the same colors

After the guests had arrived, Debbie gave each guest a paper basket.

"We are going to look for spring flowers," Mrs. Snyder explained. "You must pick up only the flowers that are the same color as your basket. What color is your basket, Timmy?"

"Pink," said Timmy.

"What color will you pick up?"

"Pink," answered Timmy. To make sure that everyone understood the game, Mrs. Snyder asked each guest the color of his basket and the color of the flowers he was supposed to pick up.

The children looked under the chairs and in the corners of the room, calling to each other when they found a new flower garden. After a few minutes, Mrs. Snyder called the children together. Judy helped the children check the baskets to make sure that colors matched. The children counted the flowers in each basket and Mrs. Snyder gave one piece of candy for each flower in the basket. The children put the candy in the baskets and took their baskets to the room where they had put their sweaters.

WHAT SEED?

The children sat in a circle. "How do we get flowers? How do we get vegetables?" asked Mrs. Snyder.

"From a store," said one guest.

"From plants," said another.

"How do we get plants?" asked Mrs. Snyder.

"We plant seeds," said one girl.

"Or bulbs," said a boy.

"That's right," said Mrs. Snyder. "Then what happens?"

"Sometimes the wind blows," suggested one boy.

"Does that make the seed grow?" asked Mrs. Snyder. The children shook their heads. "What does make the seed grow?"

"Rain," said one guest.

"The sun has to shine," suggested another.

"Yes," said Mrs. Snyder. "We are going to play a game called WHAT SEED? One person will be the seed. He'll think what seed he is and tell us if he is a vegetable or flower. Then the wind will blow. Who can act like the wind?"

"I can," said a boy. He raced around the circle saying, *"Shuuuu!"*

"Then it will rain," continued Mrs. Snyder.

"I know how the rain goes," said Nancy who lived next door. She tiptoed around the circle with her arms extended, making a gentle fluttering motion with her hands.

"Who can be the sun?"

"I can," said Debbie. Debbie hovered over the Seed, smiling broadly, waving her arms gently.

The children decided who would be WIND, RAIN, SUN, and SEED. SEED said that he was a vegetable. He knelt down as WIND whirled around him. RAIN and then SUN came near him and he began to grow a little taller. He stood up straight and the children began to guess what vegetable he was. He wasn't a carrot, an onion, a beet, a bean, a pea, or any vegetable that the children could guess. Judy and Mrs. Snyder started to guess.

"An eggplant," said Mrs. Snyder.

"Yes," said SEED.

"We never have that!" said Nancy.

"We do," said SEED. "Daddy planted some today." SEED chose someone to take his place. Then WIND and SUN chose players to take their places.

THIS IS THE WAY WE PLANT OUR SEED

"We are going to play THIS IS THE WAY WE PLANT OUR SEED. It's like Here We Go Round The Mulberry Bush," said Mrs. Snyder. "The verses will be:

This is the way we plant our seed. (*Kneel. Plant seed.*)

This is the way we hoe the row. (*Pretend to hoe.*)

plant   hoe   pull   watch   harvest

This is the way we pull the weeds. (*Stoop. Carefully pull weeds.*)
This is the way we watch it grow. (*Fold arms. Smile with approval.*)
This is the way we harvest food. (*Pretend to pick tomatoes and put in basket.*)

A child demonstrated how the group would act out each verse. Everyone then joined hands, walked around in a circle and sang the old song:

> Here we go round the mulberry bush,
> Mulberry bush, mulberry bush.
> Here we go round the mulberry bush.
> So early in the morning.

They stopped and sang the verse.

> This is the way we plant the seed;
> Plant the seed; plant the seed.
> This is the way we plant the seed,
> So early in the morning.

They circled around again, repeating the chorus, "Here we go round the mulberry bush." Each verse followed.

BUTTERFLY, BUTTERFLY

Equipment: colored handkerchief

The children, Judy, and Mrs. Snyder sat in a circle. They learned this little chant:

Butterfly, butterfly, high and low.
Butterfly, butterfly, where did you go?

One child was chosen to be BUTTERFLY CATCHER. He sat in the center of the circle. Debbie produced a brightly colored handkerchief and explained that it was a BUTTERFLY. Everyone in the circle put his hands behind his back and passed the BUTTERFLY from person to person while all said the butterfly chant which they had learned. When the chant ended, BUTTERFLY CATCHER tried to guess who was holding the BUTTERFLY. If he guessed correctly, he joined the circle and the player holding the BUTTERFLY became BUTTERFLY CATCHER. If he guessed wrong, he tried again. If he failed to locate the BUTTERFLY after three guesses, he chose someone to take his place.

BUTTERFLY HEADPIECES

"Let me show you some pictures of butterflies," said Mrs. Snyder as she opened an encyclopedia to a page picturing butterflies and moths.

"I like this one," said Timmy, pointing to one picture.

"Let's color butterflies," suggested Mrs. Snyder.

With the help of the little children, Mrs. Snyder and Judy set up card tables, covered them with newspaper, and put crayons on each. Mrs. Snyder opened the book and placed it where all could see the pictures of butterflies and moths, and then gave each child a precut butterfly (below). While Judy helped the children select colors, Mrs. Snyder excused herself and put the food on the luncheon table.

After a child had finished coloring a butterfly, Judy helped him staple it onto a construction-paper band. Mrs. Snyder returned to the living room, fitted the band to the child's head, and stapled the ends

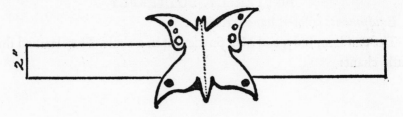

together to form a crown. Some of the children drew pictures of butterflies while others were finishing their crowns.

"Let's clean up everything," suggested Mrs. Snyder. Everyone helped to pick up scraps, put away materials, and fold the card tables.

"Now, let's fly like butterflies," said Mrs. Snyder. With Debbie leading the way, the children extended their arms like wings, and "flew" round and round the room, and into the dining room.

REFRESHMENTS

At each place was a package of easy-to-grow flower seeds, standing in a green construction paper base.

"Looks like a flower garden," said Nancy."

"The cake looks like a garden too," said one of the boys, looking at the cake in the center of the table.

"The food looks like a flower too," said Timmy, seeing the flower salad of cottage cheese and peaches in a little lettuce. The children were also served peanut butter sandwiches, milk, the garden cake and flower-pot ice cream.

GENERAL SUGGESTIONS

This party is planned for children four, five, and six years old. A seven-year-old could use the same plans, doing more of the directing himself. The games may be played with as few as four guests, the host and the mother.

FALL PARTY. You can use these same plans in the fall for a harvest party, changing the introduction of games to fit the season. For example, in WHAT SEED? you might say, "We see flowers in the garden. How did they grow?" The guests could make crowns of colored construction paper leaves.

GAMES. If you have a large playroom where running is permissible, or if the weather permits children to play out-of-doors, play WIND AND FLOWERS (page 84) after refreshments.

FLOWERS AND WIND

Divide players into equal teams. You can have as few as four players. Mark the center line of the play space. Mark a safety goal, called GARDEN, at each end of the play space. One team is the FLOWERS. They go to their GARDEN and decide what flower they will be: rose, or daisy, or tulip, and so on.

The other players are WIND. They stand at the center line. FLOWERS go to the center line and say, "Guess what flower we are."

Members of the WIND team call out the name of one flower and then another. When a player calls the correct name, FLOWERS run back to their GARDEN. WIND members chase them. Anyone who is caught, before he gets back to his GARDEN, joins the opposite team. The WIND team then becomes FLOWERS and chooses a new flower for the others to guess. The game continues until all players are on one team, or everyone is tired of running.

FLOWER SALAD

Materials: cottage cheese, canned peaches, celery or carrot strip, lettuce

Put a tablespoon of cottage cheese in the center of a plate. Arrange five slices of canned peaches around the cheese, like petals of a flower. Add a sliver of celery or a carrot strip for a stem and a little lettuce for leaves. Don't put salad dressing or mayonnaise on the salad, as many children don't like it. Serve it in an extra dish.

GARDEN CAKE

Materials: loaf cake with chocolate frosting, toothpicks, small pictures of flowers, string, plastic garden tools

This cake looks like a newly planted garden with rows and markers. Paste small pictures of flowers on colored toothpicks which will mark the rows on the cake. This can be done days or weeks before the party.

Bake the cake in a shallow pan. Frost it with chocolate icing. Place the markers at intervals on the sides of the cake. Stretch string across the cake, from marker to marker. If you wish, place a miniature plastic hoe, rake, and shovel in the frosting near one end of the cake.

FLOWER-POT ICE CREAM

Materials: small lollipop, three green gumdrops, pipestem cleaners, aluminum foil, ice cream in cup

Put three small gumdrops on the ends of three pipestem cleaners. Twist the free ends of the pipestem cleaners around a small lollipop to look like a flower with green leaves. Wrap the stem of the lollipop flower in aluminum foil. Keep it clean.

When it is time to serve dessert, insert the FLOWER in the center of a paper cup of ice cream. Be sure to serve the dessert on a plate so that the guest may take this FLOWER out of the pot and set it on the plate before he eats it.

VARIATION. Experiment with these FLOWERS before the party. If you have very small lollipops, you may want to twist three of them together with wire to make a cluster of flowers with little green leaves.

WHEELBARROW INVITATION

Materials: construction paper, writing paper, clean corner of used envelope, paste, crayons

The body of this wheelbarrow invitation is a clean corner of a used envelope. Mark up 1½ inches on one side of a corner of the envelope and 3 inches along the bottom. Draw a rounded line connecting the two dots in the shape of a fancy wooden wheelbarrow. Cut on this line through both sides of the envelope.

Cut the following from construction paper: a wheel, two handles, two legs. Cut a background piece of paper that will fit into the envelope you plan to use. Arrange the pieces of wheelbarrow on the paper. The back leg and the back handle look shorter than the ones closer to you. Paste the pieces of the wheelbarrow in place. Write a note inviting a guest to the party. Fold it in fourths. Slip it between the two sides of the envelope-wheelbarrow. Decorate the side of the wheelbarrow with a flower or design if you wish.

BASKETS

Materials: construction paper, paste

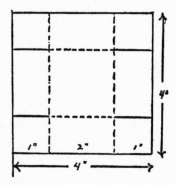

Mark a square piece of paper as shown. Be sure that all sides are even. Cut on the solid lines and fold on the broken lines. Paste the corner squares to the sides of the basket. Cut a paper handle. Paste the ends of the handle to the sides of the basket.

BUTTERFLY CROWN

Materials: construction paper, staples

Cut two 2-inch strips the length of a piece of construction paper. Staple them together to make one long 2-inch strip.

Take a piece of construction paper about 4½ inches long and 6 inches wide (one fourth of a sheet of paper). Fold it in half to make a piece of paper about 3 inches wide and 4½ inches long. Cut out half of a butterfly, with center of butterfly on fold. Open the paper.

After a guest has colored his butterfly, staple it onto the center of the construction-paper band. Fit the band to his head. Overlap the ends of the band and staple in place.

FLOWER STAND

Materials: construction paper, package of seeds

This stand will help any paper figure with a flat bottom to stand. Measure a 1½ inch strip on the long side of a piece of construction paper. Cut it off. Fold one end of the strip down 1 inch. Fold the remainder of the strip back and forth like a fan. Holding the folded strip together with one hand, slash down ½ inch in center of strip, across the folds. Fit the bottom of the package of seeds into slits.

Go West Party

"What are you doing with those little maps of the United States?" asked Peggy Slade, glancing over the shoulder of her brother Jim.

"Wait and see," said Jim as he drew an arrow pointing west across the center of the map and wrote beneath it, "Go West." He opened the paper and started to print, "Party."

"Jim, you are giving a 'Go West Party!' When?"

"Wait and read," he answered and continued to print the time, date, his address and his name (below).

"Am I invited?" asked Peggy.

"Oh, sure," said Jim. "We men folks need women folks, but do you need a special invitation?"

"Not a written one," said Peggy. "But I bet you could use a special hostess." Right then and there brother and sister started to prepare for a Go West Party which would start in their own back yard. When friends answered invitations, Peggy and Jim asked them to wear dungarees or other play clothes to the party.

GO WEST

STARTING POINT STUNTS

"Howdy, folks," said Jim as he greeted his guests. "How about keeping trim while you wait for the wagon trains to assemble.

STOOP BROTHER. *Equipment:* wad of paper for each player, table, stool, low box, brick

"Can't tell what awkward positions you'll get into," said Jim, "so better keep your balance. Tom, try this." Jim gave directions as Tom illustrated the stunt.

Jim put a wad of paper on a table near the edge. "Now," he told Tom, "take hold of your left ear with your right hand. Reach behind with your left hand and take hold of your right foot. Bend over, pick up the paper with your mouth, and stand up without losing your balance." This was easy for Tom. Jim put the paper on a chair, then on a box lower than the chair, then on a brick. Tom was very agile. He could pick up the paper from the brick. Jim put the paper on the ground, but Tom couldn't get it there.

Other guests tried the stunt, each with a clean wad of paper. Some couldn't pick up the paper from the box. Only a few could pick it up from the brick.

BOTTLE FISHING. *Equipment:* empty pop or catsup bottle, canning-jar rubber, 2-foot stick, 20-inch string

"Perhaps you can catch fish on your way West, but you may have to do it in new ways," said Peggy to some guests who had had a turn doing STOOP BROTHER. "Jane, see how long it takes you to do this."

Peggy gave Jane a stick with a string attached to one end. A canning-jar rubber was tied to the other end of the string. Peggy set an empty catsup bottle in front of Jane and asked her to see how long it would take her to get the ring over the neck of the bottle.

STORK WRESTLING. "Might like to wrestle while you wait for the scouts to report. Try this," suggested Jim. He asked two boys to pair off and stand facing each other. He directed each to stand on his right leg, lift his left leg, and hold his left ankle with his left hand. Boys grabbed right hands and pushed each other until one lost his balance. Only guests who liked to wrestle tried this stunt. Others watched.

WAGON-TRAIN TEAMS

Equipment: slips of paper with names of scouts on them, an equal number for each team

"Time to form wagon-train teams!" Jim announced. He chose guests who had excelled in the balancing, fishing, and wrestling contests to be wagon-train scouts, JIM BRIDGER, JED SMITH, and KIT CARSON.

"JIM BRIDGER, will you call your wagon train together with your long yell?" asked Jim. "Go ahead," he urged when his guest hesitated. "Any kind of yell."

JIM BRIDGER let out a "Yo-ho" holler.

"Everybody try it," suggested the host. He then asked JED SMITH and KIT CARSON to give different yells. Other guests practiced these yells too.

"I am giving you the name of the scout who will lead your wagon train. Please don't tell what is on your paper," said Jim as he handed each of the guests who was not a scout a slip of paper on which was written the name of one of three famous scouts. He also handed a slip to Peggy and kept one for himself. There were an equal number of slips for each name.

"Stand where you are," directed Jim. "Now everyone walk as far as you can while I count ten. 1-2-3-4-5-6-7-8-9-10. Stop! You are scattered. You each know the name of your scout, but he doesn't know who is on his wagon team. He has to locate you. What was your yell, JIM BRIDGER?"

JIM BRIDGER gave his yell, followed by KIT CARSON and JED SMITH, who each gave his.

"When I say 'Yell!'" continued Jim, "everyone will yell like his scout and each scout will locate the members of his team by recognizing the yell. When a scout finds you, stop yelling and help him get his team together."

SCAVENGER HUNT

Equipment: for each team—large sack containing three small sacks, pencil, list of items

"We have our teams, but we don't have any gear," Jim said when all the teams were formed. "So we are going on a scavenger hunt. The rules are simple: a grownup will go with each team; teammates must stay together; teammates will go only to the home of friends and families; every object must be obtained in the order given; no two objects may be obtained from the same house; the place of finding must be recorded; and everyone must be back here within half an hour whether the team has completed the list or not."

He gave each SCOUT a big paper sack in which there were three small sacks labeled "salt," "flour," "leavening." He then gave each Scout a pencil and the following list:

Some salt

Some flour

Some leavening (Don't bring your Mother's sourdough even if she has some. It's too precious.)

Some cotton material

A big nail

Some vegetable seeds

Something that is pretty that will not break, that isn't really valuable, and which will make you think of home.

A much-used frying pan from the home of someone attending the party

A good-luck penny.

JIM BRIDGER's team started off pell-mell to get the first thing on the list; but JED SMITH said, "We have to get things from different houses. Let's see if there is anything hard to find on the list and plan where we'll get it. What is 'something pretty that won't break, isn't valuable, but makes you think of home'?"

"Costume jewelry," suggested one of the girls. "Let's get that at my house."

"A much-used frying pan!" read one of the boys. "How about the one we take camping?"

"Perfect!" said JED. "The rest is easy. Let's go to the closest place for salt." Off the team started.

As the teams returned, the SCOUTS handed the bags to Mrs. Slade who started each group working on a NUGGET pile.

NUGGET PILE

Equipment: drinking glass filled with peanuts for each team—an equal number of peanuts in each glass; pencil and score card for each team

The gold nuggets were peanuts in a drinking glass. A player turned glass over so that the NUGGETS fell in a heap. He tried to see how many NUGGETS he could pull away from the pile without disturbing other NUGGETS in a pile. The SCOUT kept score for each team. Everyone tried his luck.

PRIZES

When everyone had returned and had "made his pile" of peanut nuggets, Mrs. Slade called the groups together to examine the GEAR. Every item was checked, and she made sure that the material collected was cotton, and not some new fabric. Jim gave a Conestoga-wagon favor filled with raisins (page 96) to each member of the team which had returned first. Mrs. Slade examined the frying pans to see which was the most used, and members of that time also received favors. She also selected the shiniest penny and gave members of the third team favors.

Jim marveled that each team had won on some score and secretly felt that his mother would have discovered something special about each bag of gear to make sure that each guest would receive a favor.

Jim checked the peanut NUGGET scores and gave a bag of candy wraped in gold paper to the winner.

INO'S REWARD

"Not all the pioneers went West in wagon trains," said Jim. "Sit down and hear the tale of *Ino's Reward.*"

Jim gave each guest a filing card on which nouns were written. He read the story until he came to the first blank. He paused as the first player read the first word on his card. When he came to the second blank, the second player read his first word. The game continued to end of the story.

This is the story of *Ino's Reward.*

When Ino Smulch headed way out West
He took the things that he liked best:
A ———, a ———, and a ——— he put in a sack.
A ———, a ———, and a ——— he strapped on his back.
Said he, "I'm going to pan for gold.
There's lots in the Western hills, I'm told."
He walked and walked, passed a ——— and a ——— on the way,
And slept at night in a pile of ——— and hay.
At the Mississippi, he hailed a ferry.
"Can't take you," said the man, "a ——— and a ——— is all I carry."
So Ino turned north and walked up stream.
At night he lay down and had a dream.

He saw in the moonlight a maiden fair
With a ——— and a ——— in her raven hair.
Around her neck was a ——— and a Canadian thistle.
In her mouth was a ——— that made her whistle.
She wore a ——— on her bright red gown,
And waved a ——— up and down.
She danced with a ——— in the light of the moon.
Ino blew on a ——— and it played a tune.
He worked in the morning feeling like a lark
And walked on up to Itasca Park.
He threw a ——— in the air and cried, " Yip! Yippy!
I can step across the Mississippi.
To celebrate I'll make a stew.
My good Ma says anything will do."
So into the pot he put a ———, a ———, a ———, and an old fish hook
And started the wonderful mess to cook.
One sniff of the stew, Ino picked up shovel and gun
A ———, and a ——— and started to run.
He ran south and west to Gold Pan Gulch;
But in the dark he couldn't see much,
Except a ——— and a ——— and an empty shack.
"Here's where I'll stay." He put down his pack,
And fell asleep with a ——— at his feet,
A ——— for a pillow and a ——— for a sheet.
He waked to hear, "Just look at his loot!
A ———, a ———, a ——— and a horn to toot."
Ino left the cabin and followed the gulch.
He figured the loot wasn't worth much.
He got out his rigging to pan for gold.
Saying "There's lots to be had in these hills, I'm told."
But what did he see coming down the stream?
A ———, a ———, a ———, and a bottle of cream.

Then he thought of the robbers. "They didn't get much,
But should we have men like that in the gulch?"
Slowly he made his way toward town,
Bumped into a ——— and a ——— and knocked them down.
He found the sheriff perched on a chair
Eating a ———, a ———, a ——— and an over-ripe pear.
Ino told the sheriff all the things he'd seen.
Sheriff said, "I reckon those men are mean.
A ———, a ———, a ———, and a ——— were stolen from here.
We'll get those men and they'll pay dear!"
So they got out a posse, surrounded the shack,
And tied up the robbers, hands at their backs.
Said the sheriff, "My men, just look here!
A ———, a ———, and a ——— that the towns folk hold dear."
Ino didn't get gold, but he got his reward,
A ———, a ———, a ——— and a Model T Ford.
If you liked this story, young ladies, young men,
Shuffle your cards and play it again.

CAMPFIRE SUPPER

"Come and eat!" called Peggy who had been helping her mother.
Guests gathered around a big pot and were served hot buffalo meat stew
(that tasted just like beef), prairie stalks (celery, tame, of course),
biscuits (sour dough, Mrs. Slade suggested), and buffalo milk which
tasted just like cow milk, and for dessert, cross-the-river rafts (ice
cream sandwiches).

"Pioneers used to sing around the campfire," suggested Jim as guests
were munching on dessert. "Let's all sing *Clementine*." One song
followed another.

When it was time to go, each guest received a miner's bag (page 97)
filled with gold candy as a souvenir of the party. It was really a ditty
bag. "Handy if you go West—or East—or anywhere," said Jim.

"One more stunt," said Mrs. Slade. "Each team must return the frying pan, the keepsake, and the lucky penny to the families that loaned them. Go as a team and an adult will go with you. Good-bye and good luck."

GENERAL SUGGESTIONS

This party is for children who are old enough to read, about seven years and up. The opening back-home games should be stunts to fill in time while guests are arriving, not rigid contests. They can be run simultaneously to keep boys and girls busy and interested. Don't insist that every guest take part in every stunt.

You do not need to have three scavenger-hunt teams. You can have two, four, or more, depending on the number of guests. You can have as few as three people on a team; but limit the number on a team to five or six, even if an organization is giving the party. Ask an adult in advance to go along with each team.

INDOOR SCAVENGER HUNT

Equipment: pictures from magazines

If weather does not permit a regular scavenger hunt, you can quickly plan one for a recreation room or gym. Cut out pictures of things a pioneer family might need for a trip West: blankets, jackets, and so forth. Make a list for each team and cut out duplicate pictures from magazines and mail-order catalogues. Hide the pictures in more or less plain sight around the room. Each team must bring back a complete set of pictures. This type of hunt does not need an adult supervisor for each team.

INVITATIONS

Materials: paper

Fold a 6-inch square of paper. With the fold at the top of the paper, trace an outline map of the United States on the outer sheet. Draw an arrow across the map and write, "Go West" beneath it.

On the inside sheet, write "Party" and give the name of the host, his address, and the time and date of the party.

VARIATION: Instead of drawing a map, draw a compass with an arrow below it, pointing West.

CONESTOGA-WAGON FAVORS

Materials: pocket-sized box of raisins, white paper, crayons, four milk-bottle tops, pipestem cleaner, glue

Cut a piece of paper 3 inches wide and 6 inches long. Glue the ends of the paper onto the sides of the box, forming a cover over the top of the box. Fold a pipestem cleaner in half. Insert the ends under the bottom flap of the box to make a tongue for a covered wagon. Glue milk-bottle tops in place for wheels. Draw rims and spokes with crayons.

If the guests are careful, they can open the top of the box, which is now the back of the covered wagon, and take out the raisins without ruining the favor.

CONESTOGA-WAGON PLACE CARD: If you serve your guests at a table, you can use these toy wagons as place cards and give different prizes. Write the name of a guest on one side of the white paper, a little below the center, before you paste it onto the box.

CARDS FOR INO'S REWARD

Materials: twenty-seven filing cards

Write three nouns on each card. You can make up your own list, using any fifty-one nouns except people. Or you can use this list: ostrich, box of matches, mice, watermelon, old shoe, Tom cat, rusty nail, baboon, rat, chocolate cake, rattlesnake, marmalade, old straw hat, featherbed, football, bunch of carrots, ox, jelly beans, pet raccoon, pair of false teeth, rhinoceros, oak tree, muskrat, cow, battle ax, horse, gasoline station, shotgun, cream chocolate, haunted house, pigeon, curly hair, car battery, chicken feather, pound of lard, gooey lake bottom, sauerkraut, codfish, baloney, catbird, sausage meat, parrot, dusty road, egg beater, long grey beard, wet blanket, squeaky door, electric train, arithmetic problem, fat spider.

If you want to play the game more than once, shuffle the filing cards and redeal.

MINER'S DITTY BAG

Materials: heavy cloth 12 inches wide and 10 inches long, thread, cord or tape

Miners often carried their gold nuggets in small pouches that look like ditty bags in which sailors carry small articles, such as thread, flashlight batteries, and so on. You can buy a ditty bag at an army and navy outlet store, or a store that handles scouting supplies. Or you can make one out of sturdy cotton material.

Cut a piece of material about 12 inches wide and 10 inches long. If you see that so-called "36-inch material" is not quite that wide, cut the width of the material in thirds which will make each piece a little less than 12 inches wide.

Make a 1-inch hem on the 10-inch side. Fold the material in half so that you have a piece about 6 inches wide and 8¾ inches long. Sew together the open end and the open side below the hem. Cut along the folded side from the top of the bag to the hem.

Cut two pieces of cord, each 16 inches long. Using a closed safety pin as a needle, put one piece of the cord into the hem. Tie the ends together. Put the other piece of cord through the hem. Tie the ends. Take hold of one piece of cord on one side of the bag and the other piece of cord on the other side of the bag. Pull them for drawstrings.

CIRCUS PARTY

A jolly clown, carrying a big sign, brought the invitation to Billy Ward's Circus Party (below). Big sister Sue had cut the clown's head and body, hat, the arm that shows, and legs from different pieces of construction paper. Billy had fitted them together like a puzzle and pasted them onto a background. Sue had added the sign that gave the information for the party.

"Mom and I will dress like clowns so that we can help you," said Sue after the invitations had been mailed.

"Good," said Billy. "A circus needs clowns, but what about animals? A circus has animals."

"We'll use your stuffed ones and pretend they're fierce. I'll make signs, like a real circus." Sue, Billy, and Mom made lots of plans for the party. At last the day arrived.

THIS WAY FOLKS

"Welcome to the Big Top," said Clown Mom as she greeted guests with Billy.

"This way, folks," called Clown Sue. "See the fiercest animals on earth!"

"Just pretend they're fierce," whispered Bill. The guests put on a big act as they copied Billy, pretending to be afraid of the stuffed lion and tiger, caged under a chair.

HIDDEN MENAGERIE

Equipment: construction paper figures of elephant, lion, bear, seal, fat lady

"I'd like to show you the menagerie," said Clown Mom when all the guests were present, "but the animals and the fat lady ran away. You will have to look for them. They are paper. They are hidden in plain sight, but they are hard to see. First look for a lion. Remember only a lion. When you see a lion, don't tell where it is. Go to Billy, sit down and growl like a lion."

"Like this," said Billy. *"Grrrr!"*

"Keep looking until everyone has found the lion. If you see another circus animal, don't say a word. Just find the lion."

The guests looked and looked, but couldn't see the lion. At last one boy spotted the yellow beast resting on the yellow cover of a book. He crossed the room, sat next to Billy, and growled. Soon everyone was sitting near Billy.

"Now we'll find an elephant," said Mom.

"He walks like this," said Billy.

The elephant was on a gray pillow. They later found a seal, which was on the black-covered telephone reminder; a brown bear, which was in a corner on the floor; and a fat lady, who was standing next to the drapes. Her dress was the same color as the drapes.

THE CLOWN IS IN THE RING

"Time to make the circus ring," said Mom. "Everyone sit in a circle." Sue helped the guests make a circle that was almost round.

"We are going to sit in this circle and play The Clown Is in the Ring. We'll sing the same tune as The Farmer in the Dell, and change the words a little." She sang the song for them; and then everyone sang it together, without any acting.

> The clown is in the ring,
> The clown is in the ring.
> Hi, ho! It's circus time.
> The clown is in the ring.

"How would a clown go around a circle?" asked Mom.

"I know," volunteered Billy. "He demonstrated a big jolly clown, walking around a circus ring, nodding to everyone.

"The clown will take an elephant," said Mom, "the elephant will take a pony. The pony will take a seal. The seal will take a tightrope walker. The tightrope walker will take a monkey." Different children demonstrated how each performer would go around a circus ring.

"You are wonderful actors," said Mom. "When you are chosen, remember who you are. Billy, you may be the clown." Everyone joined in the singing and acted out the song this way.

The clown is in the ring.
(CLOWN *walks around circle, acting funny.*)
The clown is in the ring.
Hi, Ho! It's circus time!
The clown is in the ring.
The clown takes an elephant.
(*He takes* ELEPHANT *who walks around, swinging one arm like a trunk.*)

The clown takes an elephant.

Hi, ho! It's circus time.

The clown takes an elephant.

The elephant takes a pony.

(*He takes* PONY *who trots around circle. Song continues as before.*)

The pony takes a seal.

(*He takes* SEAL *who makes noises and flaps arms like flippers.*)

The seal takes a tightrope walker.

(*He takes a* TIGHTROPE WALKER *who walks around doing balancing act.*)

The tightrope walker takes a monkey.

(*He takes* MONKEY *who hops around circle.*)

The monkey stands alone.

(*All children except* MONKEY *clap during this verse. Skip this part if children
are little and* MONKEY *seems afraid.*)

Hi, ho! It's circus time.

The monkey stands alone.

The clown leaves the ring.

(CLOWN *returns to place in circle. Finish verse as before.*)

The elephant leaves the ring.

(ELEPHANT *returns to circle.*)

The pony leaves the ring.

(PONY *returns to circle.*)

The seal leaves the ring.

(SEAL *returns to circle.*)

The tightrope walker leaves the ring.

(TIGHTROPE WALKER *returns to circle.*)

The monkey leaves the ring.

(MONKEY *returns to circle.*)

"Everybody clap," said Mom. Everybody clapped hard.

LOST JOCCO

Equipment: blindfold, bell

The players stayed in a circle while Mom explained that Bopo, the clown, was having trouble finding Jocco, his monkey.

She chose one player to be BOPO and tied a big handkerchief around his eyes for a blindfold. She chose another player to be JOCCO and gave him a little bell.

BOPO and JOCCO moved around inside the circle. When BOPO called, "JOCCO!" JOCCO stood still and rang his bell. He couldn't take another step, but he could dodge and bend and twist this way and that as BOPO came closer. JOCCO rang his bell each time BOPO called, "JOCCO!" At

last BOPO caught JOCCO. Then each chose another player to take his place.

BOPO, THE CLOWN WHO WAS TIRED OF BEING FUNNY

"We are each of us going to be Bopo," said Mom." I am going to tell a story, and I want each of you to do just as Bopo does in the story. Just copy me.

"Bopo was a clown, a very funny clown, until the day when he grew tired of being funny.

" 'Why should I be funny?' he asked himself. 'Why should I make other people laugh? Why can't I be sad like everybody else?'

"He sat down on the floor in a lump. (*Sit in a lump.*) He crossed his legs. (*Cross legs.*) He drooped his head. (*Droop head.*) Suddenly his head seemed very heavy. He decided to prop it up. He put his left fist under his chin. (*Put left fist under chin.*) That wasn't comfortable. So he changed and put his right fist under his chin. (*Put right fist under chin.*) That wasn't comfortable either, so he put his hands in his lap. (*Drop hands into lap.*) The ground was getting hard, so he moved a little to his left. (*Move to left.*) That wasn't any better, so he moved a little to his right. (*Move to right.*) He wasn't comfortable and he wasn't happy!

"Suddenly he heard music. He sat up straight. (*Sit up straight.*) He put his hand to his ear. (*Put hand to ear.*) 'Circus music!' he said. He jumped up. (*Jump up.*) He clapped his hands in front of him. (*Clap hands in front.*) He clapped his hands above his head. (*Clap hands above head.*) He waved his arms this way and that. (*Wave arms in different directions.*) As the music grew louder, he began to keep time with his feet, left, right, left, right. (*March without advancing.*)

" 'Oh boy!' he cried. 'It's fun to be happy! Bring on the show!'

"He clapped his hands three times. One, two, three. (*Clap hands, one, two, three.*) In came the show with Bopo, marching next to a donkey, left, right, left, right." (*March in position.*)

CIRCUS PARADE

"Let's join the parade," suggested Sue as she turned on the record player.

"Put on these clown hats," said Billy as he gave each guest a tall paper hat (page 107). Mom excused herself and went to the kitchen. Around and around the room the children marched. At last Billy led them into the dining room.

CIRCUS TABLE

The table was centered with a merry-go-round cake with animal crackers marching in a circle in the frosting. An elephant place card (page 108) marked each place and a brightly colored balloon floated from the back of each chair. A circus-tent napkin covered each plate. When the guests were seated, off came the napkins. On the plates were assorted sandwiches cut in triangles.

"They look like circus tents, too," said Billy.

"Fresh lemonade," said Mom, as she filled the children's cups.

"Did you ever see circus-cart ice cream?" asked Sue as she helped serve dessert.

"My cart is pulled by two elephants," said one guest.

"Mine is pulled by two bears," said another guest. The cart was a slice of brick ice cream with round candy pushed into the sides for wheels. Two animal crackers were pressed into the front.

"Oh, dear," said Sue, when the guests had finished eating. "The top blew off this circus tent. Will you help me free the animals and other performers?" In her arms she carried a big round pan, wrapped in white cloth. From it extended heavy strings, one for each guest.

"Doesn't look like a circus tent to me," said a boy.

"Did you ever see a circus tent with the top blown off?" laughed Sue. "Where is your imagination?"

Mom gave each guest a string. At the word "pull," everybody gave his string a tug. Out came a beanbag-animal or clown at the end of each string.

"The balloons are for you, too," said Billy.

"This is better than a real circus," said one guest as everyone went outdoors to play with balloons and beanbags.

GENERAL SUGGESTIONS

As this party is designed for children who are four, five, or six years old, you will have to help a young host give it. He can help make the invitations, hats, napkin tents, and place cards; but it is not necessary for him to do everything all by himself.

Plan the games early. Explain them to the young host. Play them as a family. On the day of the party, the host will feel sure of himself and be able to show guests what to do.

Dressing as clowns adds to the fun, but is not necessary.

DECORATIONS: If you really like to decorate, you can turn your game room into a circus tent, draping crepe-paper streamers from the center of the room to the sides, making realistic cardboard cages for stuffed animals, and printing signs about not feeding, and so on. However, don't be disappointed if guests glance at decorations and say, "Nice," without showing that they realize how much time and effort you put into planning. The same is true of cake and table decorations. If you enjoy baking very fancy cakes, make one of the elaborate circus cakes that you can find in many cook books.

FOOD: An older person must be with little children at all times. Don't leave them to prepare food. If you place sandwiches under napkins, as suggested, you can set the table in advance. If you do not have a dining room, pretend you are a vendor at a circus. Enter the room where the party is being held calling, "Sandwiches, ice cold drinks!" For dessert serve ice-cream bars and cup cakes, with candy clown faces in the icing.

GAMES: In playing THE CLOWN IS IN THE RING with a small group, let each guest be a circus character. You can play this game with a large group just as you play THE FARMER IN THE DELL.

Change the story of BOPO, if you wish, adding any funny motions that might amuse the children. If someone wants to tell a similar story, encourage him to do so.

If one of the games seems too complicated for the guests, substitute RINGMASTER.

RINGMASTER

Equipment: blindfold

One child is chosen to be RINGMASTER. The others form a circle around him. RINGMASTER is blindfolded. Children circle around him singing, *I Went to the Animal Fair,* or some other circus song they know. RING-MASTER calls, "Stop!" and points to a player. He then names a circus performer, perhaps "Lion."

LION growls. RINGMASTER tries to guess who it is. If he guesses correctly, LION takes his place in the circle. If RINGMASTER fails, he tries again. If he misses a second time, he chooses someone to take his place.

INVITATIONS

Materials: construction paper, colored pencils, paste

Cut a piece of construction paper a little smaller than a large envelope. Design a clown that will fit onto this background. Cut out patterns for the following parts: body and head, two legs, arm that shows, collar, hat, stick for sign, sign large enough to hold invitation. Cut these parts out of construction paper of different colors. Print the sign with different colored pencils. Draw a face. Paste parts on the background.

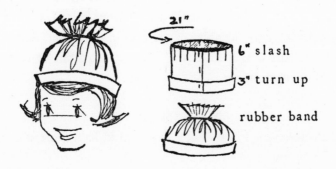

21"
6" slash
3" turn up
rubber band

CLOWN HAT

Materials: crepe paper, staples, or thread, rubber band

Measure 22 inches along the edge of a roll of crepe paper. Cut across the pack. Staple or sew the long sides of the paper together to make a tube about 21 inches around. Turn up 3 inches at the bottom. Make fringe at the top of the hat by slashing down about 6 inches at regular intervals. Pinch the top of the hat together and slip a rubber band around the paper, just below the slashes. Fluff out the fringes to make a floppy tassel.

CIRCUS BEANBAG

Materials: heavy cotton material, thread, dried beans or dried corn, magic marker, yarn or string for tail if necessary

Make a paper pattern for a circus performer beanbag. It may be the simple outline of a clown, a clown's face, or a simple profile of a circus animal. The finished beanbag should be at least 6 inches long.

Fold a piece of heavy cotton material in half. Pin the cloth together. Draw around the pattern. Sew along this line *before* you cut the material. Leave a space without stitching. Cut outside the sewing. Clip the cloth from the outer edge to the stitching at every turn.

Turn the figure right side out. Draw features or any marking with a magic marker. Fill the bag very loosely with dried beans, or with dried corn which you can usually get without cost if you live in or near the country. Sew the sides of the opening together. Sew over and over to make sure it is firm. If the figure needs a tail or mane, make one out of yarn or string.

NAPKIN TENT

Open a colored napkin so that it is folded in half. Start at one folded edge and turn the paper back and forth like a fan with about 1 inch at the bottom. When you come to the center, stop. Fold the other half of the napkin as you did the first. Open the napkin. Pick it up at the center. Pinch the center together and twist it a little. Flare the edges of the napkin out like a tent. If you wish, paste a little circus pennant on top of the peak.

ELEPHANT PLACE CARD

Materials: construction paper, colored pencil, paste

Make a pattern for a place card. Cut a piece of paper 4 inches square. Fold it in half. Open it. Draw an elephant with its legs at the bottom of the paper, its back on the fold, and its head trunk extending into the upper half of the picture.

Cut out the picture, being careful not to cut on the fold. Cut away the upper half of the paper that is in back of the head and tail. Fold the paper down again. The place card will stand up on a table.

Cut a blanket for the elephant from bright-colored paper. Write the name of a guest on it. Paste it in place.

cut away dark area

DETECTIVE PARTY

"I could write a better story than that," said Ken Blaine as he switched off the T.V. at the end of a detective play.

"So could I," remarked his cousin Dave. "So could almost anyone."

"Why don't you?" asked Mrs. Blaine.

"Well—" said the boys, suddenly remembering that to write a play meant pushing a ball-point pen, and somehow that seemed like work.

"You said that you wanted to give a party, so that your friends could all meet Dave. Why not a detective party? You two could think up a real zaney plot."

"Sure," said Ken, "about something silly, like 'Who stole Miss Peacock's antique hatpin?' "

"If we think up a plot, what will the guests do?" asked Dave.

"Mmm—" mused Ken.

"You boys think up the plot," suggested Mrs. Blaine. "Then think of a large number of clues. Write them on separate sheets of paper and put them around the recreation room. Then write more clues that have nothing to do with the plot, and put them around the room, too. Let everyone study the clues and write his story. Then have each one read his story. Last of all, read yours."

"Good idea," said Dave. "But if Ken and I are working in pairs, maybe the guests would like to write in pairs, too. You know two heads are more confusing than one."

There was no more watching run-of-the-mill plays on T.V. in the Blaine home, as the boys began to outplan the world's most hunted jewel thief and the nation's top detective.

"Why don't we have a treasure hunt, too?" suggested Dave. "You know, solve the mystery, then go find the rest of the loot."

"Good idea," said Mrs. Blaine. "You could move around after writing and listening." The boys read their story to Mrs. Blaine and told her about their other plans. After all, she was as interested in the party as they were. She offered to be chief cook for hungry detectives. She suggested that the boys include an "ice-breaker" in their plans—something to do as the guests were arriving. She didn't have to help the boys very much. They had more ideas than she did.

INVITATIONS

"What about invitations?" asked Ken.

"They ought to be official sounding," suggested Dave. "How about, 'You are hereby summoned to report for official duty as a detective at the Blaine District Headquarters, 380 Washington Avenue, Tuesday, August 24th, at 4 o'clock. R.S.V.P.'"

The boys made and delivered their invitations, plotted their treasure hunt, and planned an "ice breaker" and one game before the mystery story.

HAND PRINTING

Equipment: pencils, paper, star badge

"You know my cousin Dave," said Ken as the first guest arrived. "He's chief of the juvenile detective bureau in his home town, Pineville." "Dave, do you remember Steve Upton?"

"I remember you," said Dave acknowledging the greeting. "Will you trace around your left hand on this paper?" Ken numbered the drawing, recorded it on another piece of paper, and kept the identity secret.

After they had taken the hand prints of all the guests, Ken explained that the detectives should have a little testing before they began work on the important case before them. He asked the guests to look at each other's left hand for several minutes and then be seated. Dave gave each guest a piece of paper and a pencil. Ken passed around the numbered drawings of the hands. Guests had to guess which had belonged to whom and write down the name after the corresponding number. No one could identify all the hands, not even Dave and Ken who had done the recording; but there were some good guesses. Dave pinned a big "silver" star on the player who had the most correct answers.

MISSING PERSONS

Equipment: for each player—pin and paper with name of person on it

"Locating missing persons is always a problem for detectives," explained Dave. "I am going to pin the name of some famous person, living or dead, on your back. You must find out who it is by asking questions which can be answered by yes or no. Ask one player one question; and after he answers it, listen to his question and answer it. Don't name any specific person until you are sure you know the correct answer."

The names that Ken and Dave pinned on the backs were all well-known names such as: the name of the President of the United States, or the governor of the state in which they lived, and names of people about whom everyone had studied in history for example, George Washington, Daniel Boone, or Thomas Edison.

The guests had played the game before, so they knew what type of questions to ask in order to get the information needed to discover their identity. For example, one player's questions were as follows: "Am I a man?" "Was I ever President of the United States?" "Was I a writer?" "Was I an inventor?" "Did I work with steamboats?" "Did I work with electricity?" "Did I conduct a famous experiment with a kite?" "Did I discover an electric light bulb that would burn long enough to be useful?" "Am I Thomas A. Edison?"

When a person guessed his identity, he asked Dave or Ken to take the name from his back. The game continued until everyone had guessed his name correctly.

MYSTERY SOLVING

Equipment: paper and pencil for each pair of guests; clues all around the room

"We are ready for the mystery," announced Dave. He outlined the known facts about the theft of an antique hatpin and explained that around the room were slips of paper, each containing a clue—some relevant and some not related to the case at all. "We'll send you out in pairs for this case," he continued. He paired the person who had hand print NUMBER 1 with the person who had hand print NUMBER 3. NUMBER 2 was matched with NUMBER 4 and so on.

He then explained that couples were to read the clues, which were in no special order. Then put their heads together to solve the mystery, and write out the solution so that one of them could read it aloud. (In other words, spelling, and punctuation didn't count—just ideas.)

When everyone had either finished or given up the case, players sat in a circle. Each report was read aloud. Then Ken read the report which he and Dave had prepared. "I think the real mystery is 'How could you get so many solutions from the same set of clues?'" remarked Mrs. Blaine.

TREASURE HUNT

Equipment: clues, treasure of candy in box, jeweled hat pin

"I guess we'll have to hunt for the treasure," said Dave. He and Ken had put up the signs on the trail in the early morning.

"Hi, Dad," said Dave, noticing that his father had returned from his golf game, just in time, as he had promised to do. "We are going on a treasure hunt. Will you come along?"

"Why, of course!" said Mr. Blaine.

Dave explained that the group would go together on this hunt.

First person to find a note should untie it and hold it until everyone had reached the spot. Then read the note for all to hear and rush to the next spot. Ken read the first note.

> Don't look forlorn.
> Find a bush with thorn.

"The rose bush," called a next door neighbor.
The next note said,

> Walk east 100 paces.
> Look for a note in shady places.

This note was tied to a branch of a tree. The players continued to follow directions which took them around the neighborhood, and back to Dave's yard. There, under a canvas, was a box with a "jeweled" hatpin on the top and a final verse.

> Here at last you find the pin;
> Other jewels are within.

The finder opened the box which was filled with hard candy balls, wrapped in multicolored paper.

"Rubies," said Dave, picking out a red ball.

"Emeralds," said the girl who had found the box as she picked out a green ball.

"Now what jewel is yellow?" asked Ken, as he picked up a yellow ball.

"Melted gold," laughed Mrs. Blaine as she came into the yard, carrying a large tray.

REFRESHMENTS

Mrs. Blaine placed the tray on the picnic table. It was filled with hamburgers. The guests helped to carry out pickles, potato chips, catsup, fruit juice, paper plates, napkins, paper cups. A little later, Ken carried out the watermelon, which he sliced with care.

WATERMELON-SEED TIDDLY WINKS

Equipment: watermelon seeds, empty paper cups

"See what good shots you are," suggested Dave. "I mean with watermelon seeds. Use them like tiddly winks." He took one watermelon seed in his hand, placed another seed on the table, and tried to snap it into his empty paper drinking cup. Others copied him.

WATERMELON-SEED TOSS AND DROP

Equipment: watermelon seeds, empty paper plates and empty cups

The guests thought of other games to play with seeds. Some tossed them onto empty paper plates. Others tried to drop seeds into a cup, as they had dropped clothespins into a bottle at other parties.

Soon everyone was cleaning up. The party was over. "What are you going to do with the hatpin?" asked the girl who had found the loot. "Why not save it for your Christmas tree?" laughed Mrs. Blaine.

"That's a good idea," said the guest. Mrs. Blaine asked her to wait; and in a minute she returned with a cork, into which she stuck the end of the pin.

"If I ever need a detective, I'll know where to find one," she said as she and Mr. Blaine and Ken and Dave said goodbye to the guests.

GENERAL SUGGESTIONS

This party is for boys and girls ten years of age and over. The planned mystery does not have to be a theft; but the host should tell the plot to an adult before it is used for a party.

The party does not have to be given in the summer time; but it is an ideal time of year for several reasons. (1) Boys and girls have time to think up plots and make up clues, and time to plan a treasure hunt, make up verses and plot the course. (2) Parties planned for summer should not require strenuous activity. The treasure hunt takes place at the end of the day when it is usually cooler than at noon. Other activities are quiet. (3) Watermelon tastes best when eaten out-of-doors where no one has to be careful about dropping seeds or spilling juice.

TREASURE HUNT. Do not go on anyone's property other than your own unless you have the permission of the owner of the land to put up signs or set foot on the lawn. If you live in a city, have the hunt in a park, or confine it to your own block, so that players will not cross a street on the run.

Ask an adult to go with you on the hunt.

Write your own verses, of course!

IN CASE OF RAIN. Eliminate or postpone the treasure hunt. Bring in the box of "jewels." If you have time, play WHAT'S MISSING and TEA-KETTLE (below) tying them into the detective theme.

If you eat indoors, eliminate playing with watermelon seeds.

WHAT'S MISSING?

Equipment: tray containing twenty-five small articles such as: hairpin, spool of thread, spoon, and so on.

Enter with a tray containing twenty-five small articles. Let everyone look at it for several minutes. Take tray away. Remove one article. Return the tray. Players try to name missing article. Person who first names articles correctly removes an article for the next game.

TEAKETTLE

IT leaves the room. The other players decide upon a verb which they keep secret. When ɪᴛ returns, he asks questions which must be answered correctly by using the word "teakettle" in place of the chosen verb. For example, the players may choose "run."

ɪᴛ asks the first player, "Where do you teakettle?"

"I teakettle out of doors," he answers.

"Do you ever teakettle indoors," ɪᴛ asks the second player.

"I should not teakettle indoors," answers the second player.

"Can everyone teakettle?" ɪᴛ asks the third player.

"No, not everyone is able to teakettle," answers the third player.

ɪᴛ continues to ask questions until he guesses the verb. The player who answered last becomes ɪᴛ.

JEWELED HATPIN

Materials: corsage pin, plaster of Paris, water, sequins or glitter

Remove the cork from a pop-bottle top. This is the mold. Turn it cupside up. Sprinkle glitter or sequins in the mold. Mix a little plaster of Paris according to the directions on the package. Gently pour the plaster into the mold, on top of the sequins.

Insert the head of a corsage pin into the center of the plaster of Paris. Hold it upright until the plaster sets and the pin will stand alone. Allow the plaster to dry thoroughly. Remove it from the mold. If the top of the plaster is not entirely covered with sequins or glitter, glue some in place. Put a cork on the end of the pin until you are ready to use it.

COWBOY PARTY

Cowboys use their hats in many ways. Larry Baker made a cowboy hat invitation for his Cowboy Party. He folded a sheet of brown construction paper and drew the hat so that the top came on the fold. He opened the paper and wrote the invitation on the inside. He asked guests to wear dungarees so that they would feel like ranch hands.

- - - - - - - - on fold

RANCH TEAMS

"Howdy, Pardner," said Larry as he greeted each guest. "Here's the brand of your ranch." He gave each guest a slip of paper which had one of the two brands on it: Box B or J Lazy H (page 118). First thing on the program was a series of cowboy relays. Cowboys from Box B ranch formed one team, and those from J Lazy H formed another.

RIDING THE RANGE

"First of all, we'll have to ride the range," explained Larry. "The race is like a wheelbarrow race. The first player is the HORSE and the second the RIDER."

Team members lined up one behind the other. The leader got down on his hands and knees. He was the HORSE. The second in line became the RIDER. He lifted the HORSE's legs. At the word "Go!" they hurried to the opposite wall and back to the team with the HORSE walking on his arms and the RIDER holding up his legs. The RIDER then became the HORSE and the next player in line became the RIDER. First team to have every player race as both HORSE and RIDER won; but the contest continued until everyone had had a turn.

LASSOING

Equipment: for each team—rope tied in loop large enough to go over body of player

The cowboys then practiced working with a rope. Larry gave each leader a heavy rope tied in a loop large enough to be slipped over a player's body. At a signal, each leader put the loop over his head,

let it slip down over his body, stepped out of it, and gave it to the next in line who did the same. Team to finish first won.

DRIVING DOGIES

Equipment: potato and yardstick for each team

"Time to drive the dogies," said Larry. He gave the leader of each team a yardstick and a potato. Each leader placed his potato, or DOGIE, on the floor in front of him. At a signal, he pushed the DOGIE with the yardstick to the opposite wall, and then pushed it back to his team. The next in line did the same and the race continued until everyone had had a turn. Team to finish first won.

BUCKING BRONCOS

Equipment: gunny sack for each team

"It's time to break the broncos," announced Larry. He gave the leader of each team a gunny sack. At a signal, each leader stepped into his sack with both feet and hopped to the opposite wall and back to his team. The next in line did the same, and the race continued until everyone had had a turn. First team to finish won.

HAIL ON THE HAT

Equipment: for each team—chair, pie tin, marbles

"A cowboy's hat is a wonderful thing," commented Larry. "It gives the wearer excellent protection in a storm. This race has nothing to do with speed. We are going to see how much hail your cowboy hats can stand. The pie tin represents the hat and the marbles are hail."

The leader of each team sat in a chair and balanced a pie tin on his head. The second player stood near him and placed marbles one by one on the pie tin. The object was to see how many marbles the second player could put in the tin before it fell. No one was allowed to touch the pie tin to steady it. Every player had a turn to sit with the tin on his head and a turn to place marbles in the pie tin. Larry kept score. The team with the total high score won.

NECKERCHIEF AWARDS

"Well, pardners, you're some cowboys!" said Larry after he had totaled the scores for all the relays. "Maybe these will help you remember today." He brought out a box of different colored neckerchieves. Members of the winning relay team had first choice. "Now, you look like cowboys," continued Larry as the guests tied their gifts around their necks. "Let's see if you can sing like them."

SING PARDNER

Larry chose one player to be COWBOY. Others formed a circle around him. COWBOY closed his eyes. Other players circled around COWBOY until he called, "Stop!" They stopped. With his eyes still closed, he pointed to a player and said, "Sing, Pardner!" PARDNER started to sing a cowboy song. COWBOY had one guess to identify the singer. If he guessed correctly, PARDNER became COWBOY. If COWBOY guessed wrong, he was IT. If he failed a second time, he chose someone to be COWBOY in his place.

WHO GOES THERE?

Equipment: blindfold, chair

"All ranches have to be on the lookout for rustlers," Larry explained. He divided the players into two groups.

They lined up on opposite sides of the room. Larry placed a chair between the two lines, and chose a COWBOY to be a lookout. COWBOY sat in the chair and Larry blindfolded him. Larry motioned to a player, or RUSTLER, who tried to pass from one side of the room to the other on tiptoe without being heard. When COWBOY heard a noise, he yelled, "Stop!" and pointed in the direction of the noise. If he pointed in the direction of the RUSTLER, RUSTLER took his place. If COWBOY guessed incorrectly, he had a second turn. If he failed to point in the right direction, or if the RUSTLER crossed to the other side without being heard, COWBOY chose someone to take his place.

ON THE TRAIL I SAW

"Let's sit in a circle," said Larry. Guests sat in a circle. "Now," Larry continued, "let's think of all the things we saw on the trail."

The first player said, "On the trail I saw—" and named something, for example, a blackbird. The second player repeated, "On the trail I saw a blackbird—" and added an object, for example a rabbit. The game continued around the circle with each person repeating each object in order, and adding one more. When a person forgot an object, he dropped out of the game. The game continued until there was only one player.

CHOW

The ranch bell began to ring. Larry called for helpers and in a few seconds, tables were set up and covered with checkered cloths. Chow was served from the snack bar, labeled "Chuck Wagon." Mr. Baker served as COOKIE. There were hot dogs in rolls with brand names on top, and baked beans spooned into paper cups.

"Just like eating out of a can," remarked Mr. Baker. While the guests were serving themselves, Larry and his mother put chili sauce, catsup, carrot strips, and bottles of relish on each table. When everyone was seated, Mr. and Mrs. Baker served milk. The cowboys and cowgirls finished their meal with molasses cookies shaped like horses.

After supper everyone joined in singing cowboy songs.

GENERAL SUGGESTIONS

This party is planned for boys and girls seven years old and older. Younger children will enjoy it if they have had experience with relay races. It may be given by one person, or by a troop, den, or club.

The party may be given indoors in a large recreation room, social hall, or gym; or outside. If you are playing outdoors, substitute POM POM PULLAWAY (page 122) for WHO GOES THERE?

RELAY RACES. You can have any number of teams with from four to six members on a team. If you do not have an even number for each team, instruct the leader to take part more than once when playing RIDING THE RANGE and HAIL ON THE HAT.

FOOD. If you have the party outdoors, cook hot dogs on a grill. Serve food from a wagon marked "Chuck Wagon." Guests may sit around a picnic table, or on the ground.

BRANDING HOT DOG ROLLS. Dip a toothpick into Kitchen Bouquet or some other gravy sauce and print the brand on the top of the roll.

POM POM PULLAWAY

Establish a playing field. No one may run outside this field. Establish parallel goal lines on opposite sides of the field. You can scratch lines in dirt, mark the lines with lime, or agree that imaginary lines between certain markers will be goals.

One player is IT. IT stands in the center of the playing field. All other players stand behind one of the goal lines. IT calls,

> Pom pom pullaway!
> Let your horses run away!

All other players try to run from one goal line to the other without being tagged. IT tries to tag everyone he can. Everyone who is tagged joins IT in trying to catch more players. The game is repeated again and again, with players running from one side of the playing field to the other, until everyone is caught. Last person to be caught may be IT for the next game.

OLYMPIC PARTY

A picture of a burning torch, the emblem of the Olympic Games, headed the invitation to an Olympic Games Party which Mark Todd gave in the big recreation room of his home. The announcement said, "You have been chosen to take part in the Mock Olympic Games Party on Saturday, Sept. 12th, from 4 to 6 o'clock at the home of Mark Todd, 7832 Elmhurst Rd. Please wear sports cloths. R. S. V. P."

OLYMPIC GREETING

"Welcome to the historic games," shouted Mark when his guests had assembled. "Before we begin the contests, a word from an honored citizen." He bowed to his father.

"Young men and young women," began Mr. Todd. "May I open

our contests with the stirring words which traditionally opened the Olympic games in Greece in the eighth century.

"The eyes of the world are upon you. Your cities love an Olympic winner. From Olympus the gods look down upon you. For the glory of your cities, for the joy of your fathers, and for your own good name, I exhort you to do your best!' "

TRAINING EXERCISES

"Before we enter these contests we must get in good condition," Mr. Todd continued. He lined the guests up and had them do a series of simple stretching and bending exercises in "follow the leader" fashion.

FORMING NATIONAL TEAMS

Equipment: cards with pictures of foreign flags on them

"In this century," Mr. Todd explained, "Olympic contestants represent countries, not cities. Mark will give you cards with pictures of flags on them. Form teams according to the countries which the flags represent." When the teams were formed, Mr. Todd asked each team to choose a captain.

OLYMPIC PARADE

"Mark," said his father, "may we have a parade of contestants." Contestants formed a line, according to countries; and with Mark at the head, marched around the room.

"I now leave the contests in the hands of your Master of the Day, Mark Todd," announced Mr. Todd.

"Thank you," said Mark. "We are going to have a series of races and contests. The captain must choose a contestant for each race unless otherwise directed. Everyone must have a turn to represent his team. Each winner will score for his team. As you may know the earliest Greek races were running races. Will each captain step forward and choose someone to represent his team for the short race."

Of course, each captain tried to choose his best runner. After the contestants were lined up ready for the race, Mark explained that conditions had changed since the days of ancient Greece. In fact, conditions in the room were not exactly like those at modern Olympic games. Therefore, the races and contests which they would have during the afternoon would have the same names as modern Olympic games, but the rules would be different. The rules for the contests follow:

ONE-HUNDRED-YARD DASH

Equipment: peanut for representative for each team

Each contestant pushes a peanut across the room with his nose.

HALF MILE

Equipment: for each team—clothespin and a piece of string 5 feet long wound into ball

Each contestant has a clothespin and a piece of string 5 feet long wound into a ball. He unwinds the ball as a teammate holds the loose end. At a signal he winds the string around the clothespin.

MILE

Each team must have an equal number of players. Teammates stand one behind the other with hands on the shoulders of players in front of them. They stretch out as far as they can. The leader also stretches his arms in front of him. Measure to see which team is the longest.

LOW HURDLES

Equipment: double soda cracker for representatives of each team

The hurdle is a double soda cracker. Each contestant eats his cracker and then tries to whistle. First to whistle wins for his team.

HIGH HURDLES
Equipment: balloons for everyone
Everyone takes part. Balloons are hurdles. Contestants blow up small balloons until they burst. First to break his balloon wins for his team.

HAMMER THROW
Equipment: inflated balloon tied to 3-foot string
The hammer is an inflated balloon tied to a 3-foot string. A representative of each team holds the string by the loose end, twirls it around his head, and throws the balloon as far as he can.

SHOT-PUT
Equipment: small ball of cotton for representative of each team
Each contestant throws a small ball of cotton. The one who can throw the farthest wins.

JAVELIN
Equipment: paper drinking straw for representative of each team
Each contestant throws a paper drinking straw. The one who throws it the farthest wins.

DISCUS THROW

Equipment: paper circle, about 8 inches in diameter, for each team

Each contestant throws a paper circle as far as he can. One who throws the farthest wins. (Don't sail paper plates indoors.)

BROAD JUMP

Equipment: ruler

Everyone takes part. The first member of a team jumps as far as he can from a common starting line. Put a ruler in front of his toes. The next player of the team stands behind the ruler and jumps as far as he can. The jump continues until each team member has had a turn. The team whose total broad jump is greatest wins.

HIGH JUMP

Each captain chooses a representative. They line up facing other players. At a signal, contestants start to yell in a high loud voice. Contestant who yells longest without taking a breath wins for his team.

RELAY RACE

Equipment: book for each team

Everyone takes part. Teams line up with one player behind the other. Give each captain a book. He puts it on his head. At a signal, each captain walks to a goal and back to his team, balancing the book on his head without touching it. He hands the book to the next in line, who races in like manner. If the book falls, the player may pick it up, put it on his head, and continue to race. First team to have everyone race wins—but everyone must race.

SHOOTING MATCH

Equipment: paper bag for representative of each team

The bang counts in this shooting match. At a signal, each contestant blows up paper bag and breaks it with a *bang*. First to make the *bang* wins for his team.

TUG-OF-WAR

Equipment: marshmallow tied to 3-foot string for each player, newspapers

Everyone takes part in this contest. Players stand in a circle. Set newspapers on floor in front of them. Give everyone a marshmallow tied to a 3-foot string. Everyone puts the loose end of the string in his mouth and then places his hands behind his back. At a signal, everyone begins to chew his string. When a player drops his marshmallow, he is allowed to pick it up from the paper and start again. First player to get his marshmallow to his mouth wins for his team. Everyone keeps chewing until he gets his marshmallow.

CROWNING THE WINNERS

Teams added their scores. "Assemble, assemble," called Mr. Todd. 'The time has come to crown the champions." With great ceremony, he called members of the winning team to come forward. Mark crowned each with a paper "laurel wreath" (page 128). He gave each guest a small memento of the day.

REFRESHMENTS

"I know that as young athletes, you have been following rigid training rules, and like the Greeks of old, have been eating only vegetables, cheese, cereal, figs, and mealcakes," said Mr. Todd.

"Oh, yes?" yelled everyone.

"Now is the time to break training," he continued. "Let us dine."

Refreshments were served buffet style. Guests helped themselves to tossed green salad, half-pint cartons of milk, and casserole dishes of chicken, noodles, and peas. When the main course was over, Mrs. Todd brought in a sheet cake, decorated to look like an athletic field. Small figures (page 130) were running around the track and taking part in other field-day activities.

Laurel   Wreath

GENERAL SUGGESTIONS

This party is planned for boys and girls eight years old and older. Younger children may enjoy the contests if they are interested in track. You will have the most fun if you ask an older person to help you pretend to be serious, and then "Spoof!" Ask the adult to remain with the group at the party to act as referee, if needed.

You can give this party with as few as eight guests, four for each team. However, it is also a good plan for a larger party, such as a troop or class party. You can give it in a recreation hall, in your home, or out-of-doors. It would be good entertainment for a club picnic.

OTHER EVENTS. If you want more events add wrestling (page 88), or a chariot race run like a wheelbarrow or horse and rider race. Look in the index. You may find other contests which you can use as mock track events.

CHANGE OF NAME. If your friends are more interested in track or field-day events than they are in Olympic games, call this a mock Track Party or mock Field-Day Party.

FAVORS. The only prizes which the ancient Greeks received were laurel wreaths and the honor of winning. If your party is small and if you wish to give favors for the party, buy something that makes you think of the world, such as: small globe, a handbook of flags of other countries, or if your guests are stamp collectors, a small packet of foreign stamps.

REFRESHMENTS: If you wish to serve guests at a table, you can use the cake as a centerpiece. You can mark places with small foreign flags in gumdrop bases.

FLAG CARDS

Materials: filing cards, crayons

Choose a country for each team. Draw pictures of flags of these countries on filing cards or paper, so that each guest will have a flag and each national team will have the same number of players on it. Have at least four and not more than six players on a team.

Turn the cards blank-side up when contestants draw for teams.

LAUREL WREATHS

Materials: construction paper, staples

Cut out laurel leaves from construction paper. Staple together to form a wreath about 22 inches in circumference.

TRACK FIGURES

Materials: pipestem cleaners, aluminum foil, toothpicks

Make a number of track figures before the party day. Use one half of a pipestem cleaner for the body and legs of a track man. Use one fourth of a pipestem cleaner for his arms. Cut a ¼-inch strip of aluminum foil. Wind the strip of foil around the two parts of the pipestem cleaner.

Fold the one-half pipestem cleaner in half. Make a small loop for the head. Insert the small section of pipestem cleaner for arms between the two parts of the body. Twist the parts of the pipestem cleaner together for the body. Then separate the two parts for the legs. Bend the legs into a running position. Bend the arms. If you want to make the body bigger in any place, wind strips of aluminum foil around it.

Make figures in other positions such as throwing, or falling after a pole vault or high jump.

TRACK EQUIPMENT: Lash colored toothpicks together to make high jump bars, pole-vault bars, or hurdles.

Insert figures and equipment in frosting of cake before the party.

VARIATION: You can make larger figures for a larger cake—such as a cake for a troop—by using an entire pipestem cleaner for the body and a half pipestem cleaner for the arms. Experiment and make figures to fit your needs.

DOLL PARTY

"Look, a paper doll!" said Mary Dees as she opened the envelope addressed to her. "There's a note in the dress pocket." She showed the note to her mother.

"Sure enough," said her mother, opening the note. "Becky Lewis is having a Doll Party. The note says, 'Will you and your doll please come to my party?' "

"Which doll?" asked Mary, before her mother could finish reading the part of the note which gave the time, date, and place of the party.

"That's for you to decide," laughed her mother.

When the guests arrived, Becky greeted them, pretending that each friend was a mother, bringing a child to the party. "Oh, Mrs. Dees," she said to Mary, "how are you today? And how is Sally?" All of the guests were soon talking about their "children," complaining of colds and bruised knees, and all the mishaps that can happen to children.

DOLL SHOW

Equipment: music, prize ribbon for each guest

"Oh, my," said Mrs. Lewis at last. "I think your children look very well. In fact, I think that they are lovely. Why not have a doll contest?" Under Mrs. Lewis' direction, the little mothers lined up, each carrying her doll. Then, as Mrs. Lewis played soft music, they paraded around the room and at last set the dolls on the sofa.

"This is difficult, very difficult," said Mrs. Lewis. "It is hard to choose winners, when every doll is so wonderful." However, the guests soon discovered that Mrs. Lewis had solved the problem very nicely. Each doll received a ribbon for a very special category such as: oldest doll, most baby-dollish, most grown-up doll, most unusual doll, funniest doll, biggest doll, smallest doll, and so on.

After the dolls had received their awards, Mrs. Lewis said, "Let's clap for the winning dolls."

CLAP A WINNER

Mrs. Lewis showed them how to clap in rhythm. Then they all clapped as follows:

> One, two, three,
> (*three short claps—pause*)
> One, two, three,
> One, two, three,
> ONE! (*one big clap*)

"Let's do it again," said Becky. So they clapped again.

DID YOU EVER SEE A DOLLY?

"Let's sing Did you Ever See a Dolly?" suggested Mrs. Lewis. "It is like Did You Ever See a Lassie?"

The girls formed a circle around Becky who was leader. She decided that she would shake her wrists when they came to the words, "Go this way and that." Everyone sang and copied her motions.

Did you ever see a dolly, a dolly, a dolly?
Did you ever see a dolly
Go this way and that?
(*Make motion and continue until end of song.*)
Go this way and that way?
Go this way and that way?
Did you ever see a dolly go this way and that?

Becky chose another player to be leader. She clapped her hands on "Go this way and that." As the game was repeated, the motions became more complicated. When Mary was leader, she jumped and clapped her hands under one knee. The next leader did a squat and then stretched up high and clapped her hands over her head.

"Let's do something more quiet," said Mrs. Lewis. "The dollies must be tired from watching us."

STRINGING BEADS

Equipment: small dish, such as custard cup or individual aluminum-foil pie tin, to hold beads for each girl; beads; yard-length of linen thread for each girl; old candle

"Let's string beads," said Becky. The girls sat down. Becky gave each girl a little dish. Her mother poured unstrung beads into the dishes. They gave each girl a length of linen thread (heavy button-twist thread). There was a very big knot tied in one end of the thread. The other end had been pulled across a candle until it was stiff. Becky showed her friends how they could wax the ends of their threads in case the ends grew limp.

Some girls worked very quickly and made a string of beads long enough to go around their own necks. Others strung beads for their dolls. Some, who had made fairly long strings, wound them around the dolls' necks several times, like chokers.

When everyone had finished stringing beads, the girls looked around to make sure that no stray beads were on the floor.

DANCING LESSONS

Equipment: music

"Your beads look lovely," said Mrs. Lewis. "You look very dressed up. Wouldn't you like to give your dollies dancing lessons?"

"When are we ging to put on our hats?" asked Becky.

"Right now," answered her mother.

Becky produced a big box in which she had stored the most unusual hats that she and her mother had made.

"They look like big flowers," said Mary. They were really colored paper baking cups, stapled on a long strip of crepe paper. The girls looked gay indeed as they put the "flowers" on top of their heads and tied the crepe paper streamers under their chins. They helped each other.

"Time for the dancing lessons," said Mrs. Lewis. She turned on the record player as each girl picked up her doll and danced and danced to the music.

PAPER-DOLL CHAINS

Equipment: scissors, paper, crayons

"I think that your dolls would like company," said Mrs. Lewis when the girls had tired of dancing. She and Becky gave each girl some paper and a pair of blunt scissors. Mrs. Lewis showed them how to fold the paper back and forth and cut out a chain of paper dolls.

Some girls colored their dolls and others made more chains of dolls as Mrs. Lewis excused herself to put food on the table.

REFRESHMENTS

"Will you and your dollies please get ready for dinner," said Becky when her mother gave her the signal. After each girl had washed, she picked up her dolly. When everyone was ready, they entered the dining room.

In one corner was a doll table with cushions set around it. Each girl set her doll on a cushion and then found her own place at the dining table.

The table was centered with a big cake that looked like a doll with a full skirt. At each place sat a little doll. The girls were served Swedish meat balls, green beans, carrot strips, potato chips, milk, ice cream, and cake.

GENERAL SUGGESTIONS

This party is for girls who like dolls and who like to pretend—usually girls between four and seven years old. Keep the party small.

GAMES. If you don't have a record player or other music, or if you want one more active game, play JENNY WANTS A BABY DOLL (page 136).

If your guests can't cut well, give them precut paper dolls to play with instead of making chain of paper dolls.

RIBBONS. You can use simple blue ribbons as awards; or you can make more elaborate ones described in Space Party (page 37).

CAKE. To make the doll-cake centerpiece, use a slim doll whose body will fit into the tube of a chiffon cake tin. After the cake is baked, turn it upside down on a cake dish. Wrap the doll in aluminum foil below the waist. Fill the bottom part of the hole in the center of the cake with crumpled aluminum foil so that when you put the doll in the center of the cake, she will stand on the foil and her waist will be even with the top of the cake. Remove the doll. Frost and decorate the cake so that it looks like a lady's skirt. Dress the top of the doll. When ready to decorate the table, put the doll in the center of the cake.

JENNY WANTS A BABY DOLL

Equipment: chair or marker for each player

The game is played like PUSSY WANTS A CORNER. Every player except IT sits on a chair or stands on a marker, such as a folded newspaper or large magazine. IT goes to one person and says, "Jenny wants a baby doll."

The player replies, "Next door neighbor." IT continues to speak to one player and then another. Suddenly IT calls, "Toy shop!" At that signal, everyone must find a new place. IT also dashes for a place. The player without a place becomes IT.

FLOWER HEADBAND

Materials: three paper baking cups of different colors; length of crepe paper 2 inches wide and at least 48 inches long; glue, paste, or staples.

Find the center of the crepe paper streamer. Staple (or paste or glue) a paper baking cup on the streamer at this point. Fasten another cup on each side of the first, so that they look like flowers on a headband.

CHAIN OF PAPER DOLLS

Materials: paper, crayons

Cut a strip of paper 2½ or 3 inches wide. Fold it the short way, straight down, 1 inch from the edge. Fold the paper back and forth like a fan. Now cut out half a doll. Be sure that half of the face comes on one fold and the outstretched arms come on the opposite fold. Unfold the paper. There is a row of paper dolls.

If children are small, draw the half doll. Have them cut it out.

YARN DOLLS

Materials: cotton or wool yarn; pipestem cleaner, the same color as yarn if possible; embroidery floss

Wind the yarn the long way around a piece of cardboard 2 inches wide and 3½ inches long until you have a fat roll. (About fifteen times around with cotton twist.) Tie the loops together at the top of the card with another piece of yarn. Slip the loops off the card.

About 1 inch from the top, tie a piece of yarn around all the loops to form a head.

Bend a pipestem cleaner in half. Put it in the center of the yarn, so that the fold of the pipestem cleaner enters the head of the doll.

Wind the yarn around the short way of the card. (About six times with cotton twist will do.) Tie loops at both ends with a piece of yarn. Slip the loops off the card.

Divide the first loops below the head. Tuck the second loops in horizontally so that they form the arms. Tie yarn beneath the arm loops to form the waist. Cut the loops at the bottom of the skirt. Embroider a simple face. Bend the pipestem cleaner to make the doll sit.

PLACE CARD. If you wish to have place cards, write the names of guests on white cards. Set a doll on a corner of each card.

VARIATION. If you do not care to have a doll sit up, eliminate the pipestem cleaner. To make a pin-on doll, sew a very small pin on the back of the doll, near its neck.

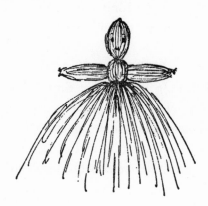

HALLOWEEN PARTY

"That looks scarey," said Ronnie Hickox as he finished making an invitation to a Halloween Party.

"And witchy, too," added his sister Joanne. The invitation was a witch's pot, filled with long white paper bones. On each bone was written a portion of the invitation which gave the time and date of the party, as well as the children's names and addresses. Below the picture were the words:

> Draw your lot
> From the witch's pot.

"What are you going to do at the party?" asked Mrs. Hickox.

"We need a ghost," said Ronnie. "I want to make a giant ghost—one that grows bigger and smaller (page 148).

"What?" asked his mother.

"Oh, you'll see," answered Ronnie. "May I use that old broom in the basement, some old sheets—"

"And is it all right if I buy sponges and pipestem cleaners," interrupted Joanne. "We want to make spiders to hang from the doorways so that people will bump into them."

"My," said their mother. "This does sound eerie!" She and the children continued to plan the party. "I knew that we built that recreation room for a good reason," she commented when she heard about the relay games and stunts which the children planned to use.

PUZZLE A TEAM

When the doorbell rang for the first time on the afternoon of the party, Ronnie scurried into a corner of the recreation room and crawled into his ghost costume while Joanne greeted guests at the door and invited them to meet the "chanting and enchanting ghost."

He was a spooky sight. His head bobbed up and down, as he grew taller and then smaller, and he swayed from side to side, repeating, "Puzzle a team. Puzzle a team."

"He wants you to draw a piece of a puzzle and form a team," explained Joanne, pointing to a bowl in which there were pieces of orange and black construction paper.

When the last guest had been greeted, Ronnie popped out of his sheets. "Match your puzzle colors and make your puzzles," he said. One team had a pumpkin puzzle and the other team had a cat puzzle. As both Ronnie and Joanne wanted to play the games, Mrs. Hickox took charge of the program.

"We are going to have Halloween relays," explained Mrs. Hickox. "The people with the cat puzzle will form one team; and the people with the pumpkin puzzle will form the other."

APPLE BALANCE

Equipment: apple for each team

"We always think of apples at Halloween," said Mrs. Hickox. "Our first race is an Apple Balance relay."

Teams lined up with one player behind the other, facing a goal line on the opposite side of the room. Ronnie gave each leader an apple and then got in line.

Each leader placed his apple on his head. At a signal, leaders walked to the goal and returned to teams, without touching the apple. If an apple fell, the player picked it up, returned to the spot where it had fallen, put it on his head, and continued the race.

When the leader returned, the second teammate repeated the performance. The race continued until everyone had had a chance to race. First team to finish won.

APPLE-AND-BEAN RELAY

Equipment: for each team—apple, dried bean, tableknife

This time a player balanced an apple on his head, held a tableknife in one hand, balanced a bean on that, and raced. The race was run like APPLE BALANCE.

SWEEP OUT THE CAT

Equipment: for each team—broom and construction paper cat

"In this relay, everyone will be a witch," explained Mrs. Hickox. Players lined up with one player behind the other, facing a goal line on the opposite side of the room. Joanne gave each leader a broom and a construction paper cat, and then got in line.

At a signal, each leader set the CAT on the floor in front of him and swept it across the goal line and back to his team. The race continued in relay fashion.

BLOW THE GHOST

Equipment: for each team—tissue paper ghost and piece of lightweight cardboard, such as shirt board from the laundry, back of a tablet of writing paper, or piece of a suit box

Ronnie gave each leader a tissue paper ghost and a piece of lightweight cardboard. The leader put the GHOST on the floor in front of him. At a signal, each leader fanned the paper across the goal line and back to his team. The race continued as a relay.

"Which team won the relays?" asked Mrs. Hickox.

"We did," said the Black Cats. Joanne gave two pieces of candy to each member of the winning team, and Ronnie gave one piece of candy to each of the losers.

SKELETON KEYS

Equipment: keys, either on a chain or in a case; chair for each player

Mrs. Hickox asked players to sit on chairs in a big circle. "Before we play this game, we must learn a ghost song," she explained. "We'll sing it to the tune of *Merrily We Roll Along.*"

Wearily we float along, float along, float along.

Wearily we float along, on this dreary night.

When everyone knew the song, the children played the game as follows.

Ronnie was GHOST. He removed his chair from the circle, walked around inside the circle with a set of keys in his left hand and his right hand extended, and sang the GHOST CHANT. He touched another player with his right hand. That player rose and became another GHOST. The two GHOSTS walked and sang together, and the SECOND GHOST touched someone in the circle. This person also rose and joined the singing and walking GHOSTS. This continued until everyone was a walking and singing GHOST. The players had chosen new GHOSTS quickly so that the game would not drag.

The FIRST GHOST led the group outside the circle. Suddenly FIRST GHOST dropped his keys. All players dashed for seats. The player left standing became the next GHOST.

WHAT WAS I?

"What kind of ghost are you?" asked Mrs. Hickox. "What did you do before you died?" She explained how to pantomime and how to play the game.

Ronnie stood in front of the others and said in a spooky voice, "Before I died I was—" He then pantomimed hammering and sawing. First person to guess that he was a carpenter did the next pantomime. If a person guessed correctly twice, he chose someone to take his place so that everyone had a chance to pantomime.

Some players needed suggestions. Mrs. Hickox whispered an occupation easy to pantomime, such as farmer, milking a cow. As the game progressed, players thought of less usual occupations, such as lion tamer and auctioneer.

TRICKS BEFORE TREATS

Equipment: bottle, slips of paper on which tricks are written

"Today we are going to have Tricks Before Treats, not Trick or Treat," said Mrs. Hickox.

Players remained seated in a circle. Joanne spun a bottle and asked the person to whom the neck pointed to choose a slip of paper from a pile, read the trick, and perform it—or try to do so.

The person who did the trick, spun the bottle for the next trick. If the bottle pointed twice to one person, Mrs. Hickox asked the player on his left to draw a paper from the pile and do the trick. If a person could not do a trick, Mrs. Hickox asked for a volunteer. If no one volunteered, the bottle was spun again to see if the next person to whom it pointed could do the trick. In the case of a fooler, Ronnie explained how to do the trick—when everyone had given up. The tricks were as follows:

INTO A BALL (*Equipment:* two single sheets of newspaper) Give the player two single sheets of newspapers. He holds one sheet by the corner in each hand and extends his arms. Now, he crumples both sheets of newspaper into balls without moving his arms or putting his hands together. (*This can be a contest if you choose two players.*)

ONE LEG BEND Raise your right leg off the floor. Bend the left leg until you are in a stooping position, keeping your right leg straight. Now, stand up without touching the straight leg to the floor.

APPLE PUSH (*Equipment:* coffee mug, apple) Set a coffee mug and apple side by side on a table. Push the apple through the handle of the coffee mug. (*After a few moments show the player how to do this. Put your finger through the handle of the coffee mug. Push the apple.*)

DIME DIZZY (*Equipment:* dime) Hold a dime directly over your head. Hold it in this position and look at it as someone turns you around several times. Drop the dime. Pick it up.

CRAZY CANE (*Equipment:* cane) Stand in the center of the circle. Put

your hands on top of a cane. Put your forehead on your hands. Look steadily at the bottom of the cane as someone turns you around several times. Drop the cane. Walk in a straight line to your chair.

FEATHER BLOW (*Equipment:* feather) Tip your head back. Place feather on forehead. Don't move your head or wrinkle your forehead. Blow off the feather.

CAN'T TOUCH Put your right hand where your left hand can't reach it. (*Trick: put your right hand on your left elbow.*)

GRAND NO-OPERA Sing the alphabet

MY FRIENDS Make a stirring speech using numbers 1-100.

JUMP OVER THE CLOTHESPIN (*Equipment:* clothespin, pencil, or ruler) Put a clothespin or some other small object on the floor. Stand so that your toes almost touch the clothespin. Bend over, take hold of your toes, and jump over the clothespin while still holding onto your toes. (*Can't be done, but a player looks funny trying to do it.*)

HIGH-HATTED WITCH (*Equipment:* witch's hat, objects which can be piled) No one had noticed that Joanne had left the room. She re-entered the room disguised as an old witch. "I can do magic tonight. I'll prove it," she croaked. "Pile things up. Make a big pile, a huge pile, a tremendous pile. Then I'll take off my hat and jump over it. Make a pile. Make a pile."

Ronnie, who is in on the joke, started out with gusto to put an empty wastebasket upside down on a straight chair. Guests soon joined him, putting books and other nonbreakable things on top of the basket.

"Are you ready," said the WITCH, looking at the pile and pretending that she was going to jump high.

"Yes," yelled the guests.

"That's a big pile," croaked the WITCH, then added hastily, "I'll take off my hat and jump over it." She quickly took off her hat and jumped over her *hat*.

"Ha! Ha!" croaked the WITCH. "Take it away. Take it away." She joined the others in putting away the things that were in the pile.

"Refreshments are served in the Witches' Den," she called as she led the group into the dining room.

REFRESHMENTS

The table was centered with a pumpkin man with doughnut eyes, mouth, and hair. A black paper cat, resting on a name card, marked each place (page 148).

For supper, the guests had "boneyard" macaroni and cheese, imp salad (page 149), jack-o'-lantern sandwiches (page 149), and witches' brew (hot chocolate).

DEAD MAN'S PARTS

Equipment: flashlight, poem, sheet, tray, and articles representing different parts of a dead man:

hair—yarn	ear—dried apricot
eye—peeled grape	brains—wet sponge
insides—cooked macaroni	teeth—kernels of corn
toes—ice cubes	liver—raw liver

nose—clay with cloves stuck in it

The party ended with PASSING AROUND THE DEAD MAN'S PARTS. Even though guests knew what was coming, they pretended to be scared. Everyone sat in a circle in a darkened room. They held an old sheet over their laps and passed around the "dead man's parts" under the cloth. Ronnie, using a flashlight, read the poem in a spooky manner. Mrs. Hickox started the various parts of the DEAD MAN around as they were mentioned.

When the night is dark and dreary,
And the sky is looking eerie,
Parts of dead men fill the air.
Sometimes you can feel their hair (*yarn*),
Or feel a damp and gooey eye (*peeled grape*),
Or their insides (*cooked macaroni*) going by.
You may get kicked by icy toes (*ice cubes*);
Tickled by a bumpy nose (*clay with cloves stuck in it*).
Here and there you feel an ear (*dried apricot*);
Brains (*wet sponge*) by themselves, feel right queer.
Teeth (*dried corn*) start to knock, and you shiver
When you feel a dead man's liver (*raw liver*);
And hear their voices, soft and clear,
"Sleep tight, young ones, for we are here!" (*Pass around tray holding all the PARTS.*)

JACK-O'-LANTERN GRAB BAG

"Reach in the grab bag," crowed an old WITCH when the lights were turned on. "Close your eyes and reach in." Each guest in turn closed his eyes and reached into the jack-o'-lantern which Witch Joanne was holding. He pulled out a noise maker.

GENERAL SUGGESTIONS

This party is for boys and girls six years old and older. It may be given at home, if there is a fairly large play room, or by an organization in a social hall. There may be as few as six children, including host. Limit a home party to twelve children.

GAMES. Children under eight years old may be overly frightened by DEAD MAN'S PARTS. If for any reason it isn't practical to play this game, substitute THE OLD WITCH IS DEAD, like THE OLD YEAR IS DEAD (page 181).

RELAYS. If a group likes a relay well, run it two or three times. Try all relays in your room before the party. You can have more than two relay teams if your group is large.

SWEEP THE CAT. In the room you are using, it may be better to have a player sweep the CAT to the goal line, pick it up, and race back to the team astride the broom. If you wish, give the leader a witch's hat to wear. He passes the hat, broom and CAT to the next in line.

TRICKS BEFORE TREATS. Be sure to try these tricks yourself before the party. The number of tricks you will use will depend on how much time you have. It is not necessary for everyone to do a trick, especially at a large party given by an organization.

FOOD. If you are having an evening party, serve only the jack-o'-lantern sandwiches, witches' brew, and the doughnuts from the centerpiece. Serve buffet style.

POT-O'-BONES INVITATION

Materials: black, orange, and white construction paper, paste
Cut a piece of orange construction paper 3½ inches wide and 6 inches

long. Cut out a big black construction paper pot, about 3 inches wide. Cut five big bones, at least ⅜ inches wide at the narrow part, from white construction paper. On each bone, write part of the invitation: party, your name, your address, date of party, time of party. Put paste around the side and bottom edges of the pot, being sure to leave the top unpasted. Paste the pot onto the orange paper. Slip the bones into the top of the pot so that they show. If you wish add this verse:

> Draw your lot,
> From the witch's pot.

SPONGE SPIDER

Materials: synthetic sponge, five pipestem cleaners, black poster paint, black thread

You can make four spiders out of a standard sized synthetic sponge about 3½ inches wide, 7 inches long, and 1 inch thick. Make a paper pattern, shaped like a spider with a large body and smaller head. Cut it out of the sponge. Paint it black with poster paint. Use black pipestem cleaners, or paint five pipestem cleaners black. Push four cleaners into the sponge in place for legs. Bend them to look like legs. Cut the remaining cleaner in half. Push it into the head for feelers and bend into shape. Tie a long piece of black thread around the neck of the spider. Suspend the spider from a doorway or a lamp fixture. See it sway back and forth with any little breeze, or when a person bumps into it.

GHOST

Materials: broom, two old sheets, construction paper, pins

Cover a broom with an old white sheet. Cut out features and pin them in place on the broom. A boy or girl also dresses up in a white sheet. He holds the broom-ghost over his head with the ends of the sheet hanging down over his own shoulders. He can make the ghost grow taller, or shorter, or wave from side to slide by moving the handle of the broom.

CAT PLACE CARDS

Materials: black and orange construction paper, paste

Cut orange construction paper unto the following pieces: base—3 inches wide and 5 inches long; ears—two triangles ¾ inches wide and 1 inch long; eyes—two small pieces. Cut the following strips of black construction paper: body—1½ inches wide and 11 inches long; head—1½ inches wide and 5 inches long; tail—½ inch wide and 5½ inches long; whiskers—three strips ⅛ inch wide and 1½ inches long.

Overlap the ends of the body strip and paste them together to form a loop. Paste the bottom of the loop onto the orange base. Press it down a little to make it oval shape.

Overlap the ends of the head piece and paste them together to form a loop. Paste the bottom of this loop in place on the body for a head. Roll the tail piece around a pencil. Pull out the pencil. Paste one end of the curled strip in place for a tail.

To make an ear, fold back ¼ inch of each triangle so that you have a piece ¾ inch high and ¾ inch wide. Fold each triangle in the center to make it look like a cat's ear. Paste in place on face.

Lay the narrow strips on top of each other and spread them out to look like whiskers. Paste together at center. Paste in place on face. Paste eyes in place. Write the name of a guest on the base of the cat.

PUMPKIN CENTERPIECE

Materials: large pumpkin, meat skewers or heavy toothpicks, knitting needles, doughnuts

Wash a large pumpkin. Put meat skewers or heavy toothpicks into the pumpkin where the tops of round eyes and round mouth would be. Hang doughnuts over these pegs. Put knitting needles into the top of the pumpkin. Pile more doughnuts on top of the needles.

WITCHES' FOOD

IMP SALAD. Make a carrot and crushed pineapple gelatin salad according to the directions on package. Cut a piece of celery about 3 inches long. Shape the top into a point. Now fashion an imp head. You can carve out the center of a white radish, carve a small piece of raw potato, or squeeze out the center of a ripe olive. Put the head on top of the celery. Insert the "imp" into the middle of a serving of gelatin.

JACK-O'LANTERN SANDWICHES. Cut two pieces of bread into large circles. Cut eyes, nose, and mouth out of one piece. Spread bottom piece with peanut butter, ham salad, cold cuts, or some other filling that will show on the bread. Put piece with cutout features on top of piece with filling.

Or make open-faced sandwiches and then add "features" made of raisins, pieces of pimento, cold cuts, or ripe olives.

INDIAN POW WOW

Fast running Kevin Davis brought the messages which invited friends to an Indian Pow Wow at his home. The message pictured a group of Indians, sitting in a pow wow as the sun had passed midday at the tepee of the thunderbird. Kevin knew that his friends would like Indian picture writing; but he wasn't certain that they could interpret the message correctly. So he also wrote, in plain English, the time, date, and place of the party as well as his name.

As friends arrived, Kevin greeted them by extending his right arm in salutation and grunting, "How! Join pow wow circle."

LITTLE BEAR IN THE WOODS

After the guests were seated, Kevin gave each one a headband with one feather in it. He explained that he would divide them into relay teams and each time a team won a race, every member would receive a new feather for his headband. Guests put their headbands on their heads and counted off to form teams.

Kevin explained that all of the relay games would tell what happened to Little Bear, a young Indian, on his walk through the woods. Everyone practiced each position for a race before the relay was run.

RABBIT RELAY

Equipment: marker for each team

The first thing Little Bear saw was a rabbit. Each player took this position: Squat with knees spread apart. Place hands on floor between knees. Move hands forward and bring feet up to hands with a jump.

When everyone understood how to hop like a rabbit, teams formed in relay fashion one with one player behind the other. Kevin placed a marker in front of each team on the opposite side of the room.

Each leader hopped around the chair and back to his team, tagging the next in line. The race was repeated until everyone had had a turn to hop like a rabbit. First team to finish was winner. Each member received a feather for his headband.

DUCK WALK

Equipment: chair or other marker for each team

Little Bear walked to a marsh where he saw a wild duck waddling along the shore. Players practiced the duck walk for which they took this position: Stoop with a deep knee bend. Place hands on hips like wings. Waddle forward.

Teams lined up in relay fashion with one member behind the other. At a signal, each leader waddled around the chair and back to his team, touching the next in line. The race continued until everyone had had a turn. First team to finish won the race and each member received a feather for his headband.

STREAM JUMP

Equipment: two balls of string

Little Bear followed the edge of the marsh until he came to a stream. He had to jump over.

Kevin laid two lengths of string on the ground, 12 inches apart, to represent the banks of the stream. Members took turns jumping with feet together across the two pieces of string. Those who jumped successfully, beyond the string, stayed in the race. Those who landed with one or both feet in the stream, between the strings, dropped out of competition. Kevin moved one length of string 6 inches away. Players who were still in the race jumped again. Kevin kept moving the string until only one player could jump across the STREAM. Everyone on his team received a feather.

CENTIPEDE RACE

Equipment: chair or other marker

After Little Bear had crossed the stream, he saw a tiny centipede crawling through the grass. Each team formed a centipede with many legs. To do this, team members formed a line, one behind the other, and then stooped in a deep knee-bend position. The leader put his hands on his hips, and each of the other team members put his hands on the hips of the player in front of him.

The object of the race was to make all the legs of this team-centipede work together so that the creature could follow a course in the race. After players had practiced for a little while, CENTIPEDES lined up on one side of the room. At a signal, they crawled around a chair in front of each team on the other side of the room and back to the original goal. Whenever a player let go of the player in front of him, or broke the line in any way, the CENTIPEDE went back to the original goal and started to race again. First team to run the course won the contest. Each member of the team received a feather for his headband.

BEES' NEST RELAY

Equipment: balloon for each player; chair for each team

Little Bear was tired after his walk, so he sat down without looking where he sat. He was a young Indian, or he never would have been so foolish. He sat right on a bee's nest and then, as you can guess, he jumped up and ran home.

Kevin gave each player a balloon to blow up. Teams formed in lines with one player behind the other. Kevin placed a chair in front of each team. At a signal, each leader ran to the chair, sat on his balloon until it broke, picked up the broken balloon and ran back to his team, touching the next in line who repeated the action. The race continued until everyone had had a turn. First team to finish won the race and each member received a feather.

VICTORY YELL

Players counted their feathers. The team with the most feathers were the winner. Other teams gave a Victory Yell for them. It went: Ki yi! Ki yi! Ki! Ki! Ki!

KILL THE RATTLER

Equipment: covered tin can filled with stones or other rattle; big paper napkins; stocking filled with other old nylon stockings

On the way home, Little Bear stopped suddenly. There was a rattlesnake in his path. Players formed a circle. One player was chosen to be RATTLER. Kevin gave him a covered tin can filled with stones. Another player was chosen to be LITTLE BEAR. Kevin gave him a long stocking filled with old nylon stockings. Kevin said it was a CLUB. RATTLER and LITTLE BEAR stepped inside the circle. Kevin blindfolded them both.

LITTLE BEAR and RATTLER moved around inside the circle. LITTLE BEAR called, "Rattlesnake." RATTLER froze on the spot and shook his tin-can rattle. LITTLE BEAR followed the sound and tried to hit RATTLER with his stocking-club. If he failed, he called again, and again RATTLER shook his can-rattle. If LITTLE BEAR failed three times, both he and RATTLER chose other players to take their places. If LITTLE BEAR hit RATTLER, LITTLE BEAR became RATTLER and RATTLER chose someone to take his place.

I SEE, I HEAR, I SMELL, I FEEL

When Little Bear reached home, his father said, "What did you see today?"

"Not much," said Little Bear.

"That's a poor Indian," said his father. "Sit down and let us discover what we can see, hear, smell and feel."

Players sat in a circle. First one mentioned something that he could see, smell, hear, or feel. Second player repeated the object and added one more item. Each player repeated all that had been mentioned previously and added a new item. No name could be repeated. However, players were encouraged to say, "Maple leaf, elm leaf," naming specific objects that were in sight rather than a general category, such as "leaf."

Whenever a player forgot what had been said, or when he could not think of anything new that he could see, hear, feel, or smell, he dropped out of the game. At last only one player remained. He was called BEST INDIAN.

FOLLOWING THE TRAIL

Equipment: small stones in bag

Little Bear's father then gave him a lesson in following a marked trail. He showed him that three stones piled on top of each other meant, "Go forward." One stone on top of another and one on the right meant, "Go right." One stone on top of another and one on the left meant, "Go left."

Kevin gave the winning team a small bag of pebbles and asked members to mark a trail. Kevin's father went with them. In marking the trail, they used stones that they found along the way as well as the reserve pebbles which they carried. Ten minutes later, the other players tried to follow the marked trail. Kevin's uncle went with them.

HUNTER, ARROW, RABBIT

While the trail markers were laying the trail, others played HUNTER, ARROW, RABBIT. Players were divided into two tribes. Each tribe had a CHIEF who decided throughout the game which pose his tribe would take. There were three poses: HUNTER (*hands on hips*); 2. ARROW (*position of shooting an arrow*); 3. RABBIT (*fists on temple, two fingers extended*). Each position had a chance to win.

HUNTER wins over ARROW because HUNTER shoots ARROW.

ARROW wins over RABBIT because ARROW kills RABBIT.

RABBIT wins over HUNTER because RABBIT runs faster than HUNTER.

Each CHIEF stood in front of his tribe and signaled. One finger meant pose HUNTER; two fingers meant pose ARROW; three fingers meant pose RABBIT. Everyone stood motionless until Kevin's uncle clapped his hands. Each TRIBE took the position directed by its CHIEF. They played this game for ten minutes and started after the first TRIBE.

When the TRIBE that had laid the trail returned, they played HUNTER, ARROW, RABBIT while waiting for the other Indians.

INDIAN FEAST

Kevin's father beat a tom-tom summoning the young Indians to supper. The table was centered with a tepee. At each place stood a small canoe (page 157), filled with candy corn. The Indians ate pemmican (meat), potatoes, wild roots (carrot sticks), berry juice (fruit juice), and corn cake (yellow cake).

After everyone had eaten and the table was cleared, Kevin announced, "Chief Thunderbird wishes to share gifts with friends." He lifted the tepee centerpiece. There was an Indian souvenir for each guest.

GENERAL SUGGESTIONS

This party is planned for boys and girls seven years and older. Younger children will enjoy it if they have had experience with relay races.

All of the games, with the exception of trail setting, may be played indoors or out-of-doors. You will have to decide for yourself whether it is practical to set a trail in the locality in which you live or on the day on which you give the party.

If you do not set the trail, have the guests string inexpensive beads or macaroni bits during the extra time. Or substitute stringing beads for any other game that is not suitable for your group or for the place in which you are giving the party.

HUNTER, ARROW, RABBIT. Players will learn this game quickly if one or two players know it well. It can be played with as few as two people, so practice it with your family and friends before the party.

If you have time, play TAKE ME TO YOUR CHIEF like TAKE ME TO YOUR LEADER (page 34).

FOOD. If your party is held out-of-doors, serve meat sandwiches instead of meat and potatoes. Eliminate the table setting and give miniature canoes or other gifts as favors.

INVITATIONS

The invitations may be made on brown wrapping paper, or they may be drawn on government postcards and mailed.

HEADBAND

Materials: corrugated paper, paper clip, construction paper

Cut a strip of corrugated paper 2 inches wide and 23 inches long. Fit it onto a head, overlapping the ends, and fasten in place with a paper clip.

Cut feathers, shaped like chicken feathers, out of several different colors of construction paper making sure the quills are long enough to fit into the holes of the corrugated paper. Or you may use real chicken or turkey feathers.

VARIATION. If you cannot get corrugated paper, make a headband out of a double strip of construction paper. Staple feathers in place.

TEPEE

Materials: brown paper, paste, crayons, twigs

Draw a half circle on a large sheet of brown paper. Cut it out. Decorate it with Indian designs. Overlap one half of a straight edge on the other half to form a cone. Paste in place. Cut a diagonal slit in the front. Turn it back like a door-flap. Put three little twigs in the top for poles.

CANOE

Materials: paper, paste, crayons

You can buy little canoes for favors, or you can make your own.

Fold a piece of paper in half. Draw a canoe with the bottom on the fold of the paper. Cut it out. Color a design on it. Write the name of a guest on the side. Paste the sides together at the ends. Flatten the bottom so that the canoe will stand.

CAR AND TRUCK PARTY

"Here's a car that fits," said Gary Ford, pointing to a picture of a station wagon in an old magazine.

"Cut it out," said his mother.

"This truck's too big," said Gary, looking at another picture.

Gary and his mother were making invitations for a Car and Truck Party. Gary chose the pictures, cut them out as well as he could, and pasted them onto government postcards. His mother wrote, "Please come to my car and truck party. Bring your favorite car or truck to play with," and added Gary's name and address and the date and time of the party.

PLAYING WITH CARS AND TRUCKS

Before the party, Gary and his mother brought the blocks, an assortment of small boxes, and some of Gary's cars and trucks into the living room. As guests arrived Gary greeted them and Mrs. Ford encouraged them to join Gary in playing with the cars and trucks, building new garages, making highways across the floor, and so on.

"How does the horn on the little car sound?" asked Mrs. Ford.

"Beep, beep!" said Gary as he pushed his little car.

"I want to make the little car go *'Beep, beep!'*" said Glen who lived next door. Gary shared his little car with Glen and Glen let Gary play with the truck he had brought.

"How does the horn on the big truck sound?" asked Mrs. Ford.

"Honk! Honk!" said Gary.

The children played with the cars and trucks for about half an hour. One boy wanted to play only with the car he had brought. Other children were glad to share toys.

"Time to pick up," said Mrs. Ford. The children put the blocks into their boxes, set the garages along the wall, and parked their cars in a straight line. Then they sat down to listen to a story.

STORY WITH SOUND EFFECTS

"This is a story about two cars," explained Mrs. Ford. "A very old car that said, *'Chug-along, chug-along, chug, chug, chug'* and a new car that said, *'Zoom!'* What did the old car say?" The children repeated the sound. "What did the new car say?" The children said, *"Zoom!"*

"I want you to help tell this story," continued Mrs. Ford. "Whenever the story says, 'The old car said,' we'll all say together, *'Chug-along, chug-along, chug, chug, chug.'* Whenever the story says, 'The new car said,' we'll all say, *'Zoom!'"* When Mrs. Ford came to *"chug-along, chug-along, chug, chug, chug,"* she tapped her foot as she said the words, to help the children catch the rhythm of the sound of the old car going down the road.

CHUG-ALONG AND ZOOM

Once there was a very old car. Whenever it went down the road, it said, *"Chug-along, chug-along, chug, chug, chug."* There was also a new car. When it went down the road, it said, *"Zoom!"*

Every day the old car went down Skillmans' Lane. When it went up the hill, it said (*slowly*) *"Chug-along, chug-along, chug, chug, chug."* When it went down a hill it said (*a little faster*) *"Chug-along, chug-along, chug, chug, chug."*

Every day the new car went down Skillmans' Lane. When it went up a hill, it said (*fast*) *"Zoom!"* When it went down a hill it said (*fast*), *"Zoom!"* It always went as fast as the law allowed.

Every day the new car and the old car parked side by side in a company parking lot.

"You go too fast on Skillmans' Lane," commented the old car one day when work was over. "Skillmans' Lane is very bumpy. Skillmans' Lane has many curves. You should slow down on Skillmans' Lane."

"Axle grease!" sneered the new car. "I am a new car. You are an old car. I can take bumps. I can take curves. I like to go as fast as the law allows. Good-bye now!" He left the parking lot saying, *"'Zoom!'*

"Good-by," called the old car. He left the parking lot saying, *"Chug-along, chug-along, chug, chug, chug."*

Now Skillmans' Lane was a country road. It was always bumpy. In summer and fall, it was bumpy and dusty. In winter, it was bumpy and snowy. In spring it was bumpy and muddy—very, very muddy—slishy, slashy, slide-around-muddy—and full of holes.

In the spring, the old car went down Skillmans' Lane very carefully dodging holes, going slowly over the bumps, and making sure not to get its wheels in the soft mud on the shoulders. It kept saying, *"Chug-along, chug-along, chug, chug, chug."*

The new car paid no attention to the mud. It went up the hill saying *"Zoom!"* It started down the hill saying, *"Zoom—Bang!"* It hit a bump, swerved into the mud, and slid into a tree.

The old car heard the crash. It hurried up the hill as fast as it could go safely saying, *"Chug-along, chug-along, chug, chug, chug."*

"Oh, dear! Oh, dear!" moaned the new car. "I went too fast for the condition of the road. What shall I do?"

"Stay where you are," called the little old car. "I'll get a wrecker to pull you out." Off he went saying, *"Chug-along, chug-along, chug, chug, chug."*

The wrecker pulled the new car onto the road. It was a sad sight, all covered with mud, its headlights broken, its fenders bent. However, its engine was still running. "Oh, thank you, little old car. Thank you, wrecker. I think I can go on." He started down the road saying (slowly), *"Z-o-o-m."*

The two cars still go down Skillmans' Lane. The old car says, *"Chug-along, chug-along, chug, chug, chug."* Sometimes it goes very slowly, saying, *"Chug-along, chug-along, chug, chug, chug."* Sometimes it goes a little faster saying, *"Chug-along, chug-along, chug, chug, chug."* It all depends on the condition of the road.

The nearly new car goes down Skillman's Lane. Sometimes it goes *very slowly saying "Z-o-o-m."* Sometimes it goes a little faster saying

"Zoom!" Everything depends upon the condition of the road.

PARADE OF CHUG-ALONGS

"Let's have a parade of Chug-alongs," said Mrs. Ford. The children formed a line and marched around and around the room chanting, *"Chug-along, chug-along, chug, chug, chug."* At last they filed into the dining room for a "Roadside lunch."

ROADSIDE LUNCH

The table was centered with a cardboard garage with paper sides. Ribbons extended from it, like highways, leading to each place.

Mrs. Ford and Gary served an assortment of sandwiches, milk and gingerbread cookies shaped like cars. When it was time for dessert, Mr. Ford entered the room ringing a bell and calling "Ice cream! Ice cream!" just like a vendor on the highway. He gave each child an ice-cream bar.

When all the food was eaten and the table cleared, Mrs. Ford asked each child to take hold of the end of the ribbon near his place. At the signal, "Pull!" everyone pulled his ribbon. Out of the garage came a toy car for each guest.

GENERAL SUGGESTIONS

This party is planned for children three, four, or five years old. In most cases, a boy would like to be host; but girls as well as boys would like to attend. Keep the party small and invite only children who play together frequently. It should not last more than an hour and a half.

GAMES. If you feel the need for additional or more organized play, include I'LL DRIVE MY CAR TO HIS HOUSE (below).

STORY TELLING. You can read or tell the story as it is without props. Or you can use variations.

Stick puppets. (*Materials:* paper, colors, paste, cardboard, lath thumbtacks) Draw pictures of the old car and the new car. Color them. Cut them out and mount them on lightweight cardboard. Thumbtack the pictures onto short pieces of lath. Hold up each picture and wiggle it when it is mentioned in the story.

Cars. Use model cars as you would puppets: a Model T or A and a new model.

Picture book. This is an easy story to illustrate. Make pages with pictures. Mount them on cardboard. Hold them up as you tell the story.

I'LL DRIVE MY CAR TO HIS HOUSE

Equipment: toy car

Children form a large circle. If only three or four are playing, have them sit far apart.

A player takes a toy car and says, "I'll drive my car to Tom's house" (or whatever the name of the child may be). He pushes the car across the circle, saying *"Honk! Honk!"* He sets it in front of the chosen player and returns to his place. The game is repeated a number of times.

INVITATIONS

Materials: magazine ads, paste, government postcards

Choosing a picture that will fit onto a card is a good experience for any young child. Let him decide if a picture is too big to fit into a given space. If there is any doubt about a specific picture he has chosen, have him place the card over the picture. Let him see if it extends beyond the card.

Don't insist that he cut out the picture all by himself. If he is dissatisfied with his cutting, trim the edges for him; or if necessary, have him cut out the part of the page on which the picture appears, and then cut out the outline for him. However, encourage him to do what he can. You might comment, "I bet Glen will say, 'Gary cut that out himself. Good for Gary!' "

Almost any child old enough to have a party can paste the pictures on the cards.

GARAGE CENTERPIECE

Materials: cardboard box, wrapping paper, paint, paste, toy cars, ribbon

Choose a cardboard box the size and shape that you want for a centerpiece. Cut out large sections of each side, leaving a framework. Paste wrapping paper around the sides. Print a sign on each side: GARY'S (using the host's name) GARAGE. Attach a ribbon to a small toy car for each guest. Place toys in the center of the table, facing out, with a ribbon leading to each place. Set the cardboard garage over the toys.

GINGERBREAD-COOKY CARS

If you cannot find a cooky cutter in the shape of a car, you can make a pattern. Draw the side view of a car, either the old one or the new one in the story. Using this as a pattern, cut out a cardboard car.

Mix dough for a gingerbread-man cooky. Roll out the dough. Put a little flour on the cardboard pattern. Lay it on the dough. Cut around it with a pointed knife. Bake cookies according to the directions for gingerbread men. Use the cookies plain, or decorate with frosting.

CHRISTMAS PARTY

"It's Christmas around the world," said the Christmas card which Taffy Jones received. On the card was a big red stocking filled with pictures of wrapped gifts. Taffy soon noticed that she could pull out the gifts. On the bottom of each was part of an invitation to Polly Dunn's Christmas party. Then Taffy noticed, "Over" at the bottom of the card. On the other side was the instruction, "Please bring an unwrapped 25-cent toy for the X Club's Christmas baskets."

STIR THE CHRISTMAS CAKE

Equipment: wooden spoon, chair for all but one player

"First we must get ready for Christmas," explained Polly when her guests were ready to play games. "In every country people do special cooking at Christmastime. The first game is Stir the Christmas Cake."

One player was chosen to be COOK. Other players sat in chairs around her. Polly gave COOK a wooden spoon. COOK stood in the center of the circle, pretending to be stirring a big cake, and saying, "Stir and stir the Christmas cake. Stir and stir—" Suddenly she dropped the spoon. This was a signal for everyone to change chairs. COOK ran for a chair, and the player who was left standing became COOK.

PEANUTS IN THE SHOE RELAY

Equipment: tablespoon, shoe, and pile of peanuts for each team

"In Holland, children expect St. Nicholas to fill their shoes," explained Polly. She divided the guests into relay teams. Each team formed a line on one side of the room behind a leader. Polly gave a tablespoon to each leader. She put a pile of peanuts in front of each team and a shoe opposite each team on the other side of the room. She explained that the object was to see how many peanuts a team could get into its shoe without touching them. Speed would count only in the case of a tie.

At a signal, each leader scooped up as many peanuts on her spoon as she could without using her hands, raced to the opposite side of the room, dropped the peanuts into the shoe, returned to her team, and gave the spoon to the next in line who did the same. The team which had the most peanuts in its shoe won. The second time that they ran the relay, there was a tie. Mrs. Dunn said that the team that had finished ahead of the other won. They ran the race three times.

BLIND MUMM

Equipment: large paper bag with funny face drawn on it for each player

"English children used to play Blind Mumm during the Christmas season," explained Polly. "It reminded them of the Mummers, people who dressed up and went from house to house singing Christmas carols."

One player was chosen to be BLIND MUMM. He put a big paper-bag mask, with mouth cut out, over his face. Other players formed a circle around him as close as possible. BLIND MUMM turned around three times. Then he counted, "One, two, three!" as other players took three steps in any direction.

BLIND MUMM groped his way around until he touched someone. This player started to sing a Christmas song. BLIND MUMM tried to guess who it was. If she guessed wrong, she was BLIND MUMM again. If she guessed correctly, the person who was caught became BLIND MUMM. Polly gave the new BLIND MUMM a different bag, and put the first bag at the side of the room. Everyone had a turn to be BLIND MUMM.

DECORATING A CHRISTMAS TREE

Equipment: two old sheets, two paper hats, many safety pins, many old cards with string attached, little bells for members of one team and snapper noisemakers for members of the other team

"Christmas trees came from Germany," Polly explained. "Today we'll have a new kind of Christmas tree." She divided the guests into two teams. She asked each team to choose one player to be its leader. Then she asked each team to choose another member to be its Christmas tree. She wrapped an old sheet around the body of each TREE and put a green hat with a star on it on its head. She placed a dish of safety pins at the foot of each TREE.

She explained that hidden in plain sight around the room were many decorations: old cards with strings attached. Polly gave snapper noise-makers to members of one team and little bells to members of the other team. The players were asked to hunt for decorations. When a player found one, he stood still and either jingled his bell or snapped his snapper. The LEADER of the team came when he heard his signal, got the decoration, and pinned it on his TREE. He could get only one decoration at a time. No player could look for another decoration until his

LEADER had collected the one for which he was signaling.

The hunt and the trimming continued for ten minutes. Polly called a halt. Everyone looked at the two TREES and tried to decide which one was prettier. They couldn't decide. Then they counted the decorations. Team with the most decorations on its TREE won. Everyone helped to carefully remove the decorations so as not to tear them. Players who had been TREES and LEADERS received bells and snappers. Guests put their bells and snappers in the bags which they had used while playing BLIND MUMM.

WRAPPING GIFTS

"A Christmas tree always makes us think of gifts," remarked Polly. She and her friends set up card tables and Polly produced the usual things needed to wrap gifts: paper, ribbon, cellophane tape, and Christmas seals. Then she added "extras": cotton, bits of ribbon, construction paper, crayons, scraps of cloth, old beads, pine cones, paste, and so on. She explained that they were going to wrap the gifts that they had brought. Polly first asked everyone to write the type of gift on one of the cards which they had used for decorating so that X club would know whether to give the gift to a little boy or a little girl, a big boy or big girl, or to a family that might like to play games.

Polly asked everyone to use her imagination in wrapping the gift. She said that they could decorate it with angels, Santas—anything Christmasy. Or they could make an unusual card for the top.

REFRESHMENTS

While the guests were busy wrapping gifts, Polly helped her mother put the food on the table. On each plate was a baked potato, frozen green beans, a red pickled apple slice, and a slice of meat loaf which Polly had decorated with a catsup bell, squeezed out of a plastic bottle. They also served milk and small rolls; and for dessert, holiday ice cream and cup cakes.

Polly and her mother returned to the living room to see the wrapped gifts. No one could choose the prettiest, or the most clever, so no one tried. The gifts were put on display and everyone helped to pick up scraps and get ready for dinner.

ROYAL FEAST

Equipment in addition to decorations: crowns for king and queen, cap for court jester

The table was centered with a popcorn-ball tree. At each place was a napkin, shaped like a Christmas tree, and a place card with either a Clothespin Santa or an angel snapped onto the top (page 172).

When the guests had finished the main course, Mrs. Dunn said, "The cake we are serving is *Gateau des rois.*"

"What?" asked everyone.

"*Gateau des rois,*" repeated Mrs. Dunn. "Cake of the kings. It's a special cake that French Canadians bake in honor of the three kings of the Orient who came to the manger."

"And the other king, too," added Polly, "the king of Christmas."

"Yes," explained Mrs. Dunn. "Usually the cake is baked as one big cake, with fortunes in it. We decided to have cup cakes, but the same fortunes are in it. Eat the cake carefully. The person who gets a bean is King. The person who gets a pea is Queen. The person who gets a clove is Court Jester." After the guests had found their symbols, Polly crowned the King and Queen and gave the Court Jester a hat with a little bell at the tip of the crown.

PINATA

Equipment: Piñata (page 174) and stick

"Time for the Piñata," said Polly when dinner was finished. "That's worth going to Mexico for." Down into the basement they trooped. A paper bag was hanging from a hook on the beams.

"Who will hit the Piñata?" asked Mr. Dunn, who had returned from work.

"I!" "I!" "I!" answered all the guests together. Mr. Dunn closed his eyes and chose a player. He gave her a big stick and then tied a bag paper napkin around her eyes. He turned her around three times, and told her to hit the Piñata. She missed. Others tried. At last, a player hit the Piñata, and out on the floor fell pieces of wrapped candy. Everyone scrambled to pick up all that she could. The guests took the candy upstairs and put it in the bags they had worn for BLIND MUMM.

WHO BROUGHT THE GIFT?

"While you were downstairs, someone left a gift," said Mrs. Dunn showing the group a big box. "I didn't see the donor. Maybe it was Cristkindli, the lovely angel who leaves gifts in Switzerland. Maybe it was the old witch La Befana, who leaves gifts in Italy. Or maybe Julenisse, a little gnome, who brings gifts in Denmark. Who else could have left it?"

"St. Nicholas," said one guest. "He leaves gifts in Holland."

"Santa Claus," said another guest. He needed no identification.

"There isn't a mark on it," continued Mrs. Dunn. "Let's take turns opening it."

The guests and Polly sat in a circle. "We'll let the King start," said Polly. KING took off the wrapping, and found another box inside. She handed the box to the next in the circle. The girls unwrapped and unwrapped. Each box got smaller. At last, one player came to the last box. In it was a small gift for each guest.

Mrs. Dunn took apart the popcorn-ball Christmas tree, put each ball in a wax-paper sack, and gave them to the guests. Blind mumm's masks turned into a carry-all sacks to hold popcorn balls, snappers or bells, clothespin place cards, extra card-decorations, Piñata candy, and the gift.

GENERAL SUGGESTIONS

This party is planned for boys and girls seven years old and older. Try to set a date early in December, before everyone is busy with family, school, and church plans.

If you are giving this party in your home, keep the guest list small. You can have as few as five guests and the hostess. This allows three people to be on a team for games, with the hostess playing and an adult leading the games.

You can also use these plans for a larger group of children, for example; a troop could give the affair in a gym or a recreation hall.

Guests must not walk home alone on a winter evening in the dark. Tell parents that you will telephone them when the party is over so that they can call for the children. Sing carols or listen to Christmas music while waiting, or ask an adult to read a Christmas story.

GIFTS FOR OTHERS. If you would like to have guests bring gifts for a charitable cause, as suggested here, first call the organization to find out just what gifts are suitable for the baskets or packages they are sending, their deadline for accepting gifts, and if they can accept wrapped gifts when they know what is in the packages.

DECORATING TREE GAME. A time limit for decorating the TREE game is given here. Don't let this activity drag. However, if guests are having fun and there are more decorations to be found, extend the time.

GATEAU DES ROIS

Cake of the Kings is a cake which the French Canadians bake for the after-Christmas season. However, it is also associated with the entire Yule season. Baked into it is a bean, a pea, and a clove. The person who gets the bean is King of the Christmas festivities. The person who gets the pea is Queen. The person who gets the clove is Court Jester. If your party is small, make cupcakes, putting one of these three ingredients into three of the cupcakes. Mark these cupcakes with toothpicks so that you will be sure to serve them. If you bake a big cake, and do not serve the entire cake, the part of the cake with the "fortunes" in it may remain uneaten.

INVITATIONS

Materials: construction paper, used gift-wrapping paper, paste

For a background, cut a piece of construction paper which will fit into the envelope which you plan to use. Draw and then cut out a big stocking that will fit onto this background paper. Put paste *only* on the edges of the leg and foot of the stocking. Leave the top open. Paste the stocking onto the background. Cut five strips of construction paper ½ inch wide and from 2½ to 3½ inches long. Cut small pieces of gift-wrapping paper and paste them onto the ends of the strips. The decorated paper should be of different lengths, to look like packages of different sizes.

Write the information about the party on the plain parts of these strips: on one write, "Christmas Party," on another the date and time; and on another your name and address; and on the last, "Stay for supper." Near the heel of the stocking write, "It's Christmastime around the world (over)." On the back of the invitation, ask friends to bring inexpensive unwrapped gifts which some organization can put into its Christmas baskets.

BLIND MUMM MASK

Materials: large grocery sack, poster paints

Paint a funny face on a large sized grocery sack. Cut out the mouth, but not the eyes. When the wearer puts on the mask, it rests loosely on his shoulders, giving plenty of air for breathing.

CHRISTMAS-CARD TREE DECORATION

Materials: old Christmas card, yarn or cord

Cut out part of a Christmas card which has no writing on it. Punch a hole in the top of the card. Put a cord through the hole and tie it in a loop.

SANTA AND ANGEL CLOTHESPIN PLACE CARDS

Materials: snap clothespins, construction paper, poster paint, glue, paste, filing card or light-weight cardboard. Paint a snap clothespin red for Santa, white for an angel

SANTA. You can make Santa's face different ways. (1) Draw a picture of Santa's face and color it. It must be as wide as the clothespin. Cut it out. (2) Make the face from several scraps of construction paper. Cut a face as wide as the clothespin from pink paper. Cut out and

paste in place white whiskers and mustache. Draw a mouth, nose, and eyes. Cut out a red cap. Add white paper trim and tassel. Paste it onto the face. (3) Find a paper sticker with a Santa-Claus face the right size. Glue or stick the face onto the red clothespin.

ANGEL. Draw an angel face on pink paper. It must be just as wide as the clothespin. Glue it onto the top of the white clothespin. Draw and cut out double wings which will fit onto the back of the angel. Glue them on the wood in back of the face. Cut out a round yellow halo. Glue it in back of the face. For a hymn book, cut a little piece of blue paper. Fold down ¼ inch of one end. Glue the ¼-inch strip onto the clothespin so that the top of the book stands out a little.

PLACE CARD. Fold a filing card or piece of light-weight cardboard in half so that it will stand alone with the fold on top. Write the name of a guest on the card. Snap the clothespin Santa or angel onto the top of the card. Adjust the card so that it will not topple over. This favor can later be used as a tree ornament.

CHRISTMAS-TREE NAPKIN

Materials: napkin, stickers

Place a folded paper napkin on a table so that the open corner is in front of you and folded corner is farthest from you. Fold the right-hand corner and the left-hand corner to the center of the napkin. Press the folds. This portion of the napkin looks like a Christmas tree.

Cut the dangling part of the napkin into the shape of a tree trunk and a Christmas tree stand. Turn the napkin over with the folds on the table. Paste stars or other stickers on the Christmas tree.

POPCORN-BALL TREE

Materials: popcorn balls, green cellophane paper, gumdrops

Make this decoration a day or two before the party. Keep it covered. You do not have to take the tree apart to give the balls to the guests; but food which serves as a decoration soon gets too dusty to eat.

Cover a large dish or small tray with green cellophane paper. Make popcorn balls, varying in size from about 2 to 3 inches in diameter. Set aside one small ball for the top of the tree. Flatten all the others a little on the top and bottom.

While the balls are still sticky, pile them into the shape of a tree. Put eight balls in a circle and one small ball in the center. Make the next circle smaller and so on until the tree is formed. Put the small round ball on top. (You can vary the number of balls to make a tree that fits on the dish you wish to use.)

Press brightly colored small gumdrops into the sticky popcorn. They will look like lights.

Cut 4-inch green cellophane circles. Put your first finger into the center of a circle. Close the paper up and around it. Press the paper near the tip of your finger. Remove your finger. Twist the top of the paper. Tuck these crushed circles in between the popcorn balls wherever there is a hole.

Top the tree with any decoration you wish.

PINATA

Materials: paper bag, wrapped candy, paint, string

You can buy a clay Piñata in some stores; but you can have just as much fun with a paper bag Piñata. Paint the face of a person or animal on a big paper bag. Put wrapped candy in the bag. Tie the top of the bag with a stout string, allowing the ends to dangle.

You can suspend the bag from a hook in the ceiling if you have open rafters. Do not put hook anywhere without permission!

Another way to suspend the Piñata is to tie the ends of the string to the center of a long rope. Ask adults to hold the ends of the rope, keeping it taut so that the bag will stay suspended. The adults must stand at some distance from the bag so that they will not be hit by the stick when a person swings it.

END-OF-THE-YEAR PARTY

Bargains of fun!
End-of-the-Year Party!

began the announcement which the Boys and Girls Club sent out. The invitation, printed on a government postcard, looked like an ad and included, besides the time and place of the party, "R. S. V. P."

"We have to know how many are coming in order to plan," said Sarah Sheldon, as she put an especially large period after the last "P." she had written.

"You know, I like Miss P.'s idea of stunts and teams," said Jerry Williams, as he picked up cards and put them in order, ready for mailing. "If everyone comes, we could have four teams—" The committee, which had been thinking in general terms, began to plan details of the party. Miss P.—Jerry meant Miss Parker—the club's advisor—had suggested that the committee look for silly contests that are as much fun to watch as they are to do. "Not everyone will take part in every contest," she had explained. "In some cases, representatives can perform a stunt, while the rest of us watch." The committee planned other activities, too, all related to the old year.

THREAD OF LIFE

Equipment: 6-inch length of thread, cord, or yarn for each guest

As the guests arrived, Sarah gave each one a short length of colored cord saying, "Hang onto this. It is part of the thread of life."

"What?" asked the guest. As Sarah was busy greeting the next arrivals, members walked around, dangling the threads, which they had noticed were of different colors, asking, "What does she mean, 'Thread of life?'"

When the last club member had arrived, Miss Parker blew her whistle. "Happy old year!" she called.

"Happy old year!" everyone shouted.

"Miss P., what does it mean 'thread of life!' " called Bobby Furman.

"The ancient Greeks believed that each man had a thread of life which was spun by three fates, and then clipped," explained Miss Parker. "Each of you received a piece of cord. You can see that there are four different colors. You are to form teams, by matching colors. Then tie your matching cords together into one long thread of life. First team to bring me one long piece of cord wins a point for his team."

SHARE-THE-FOOD RELAY

Equipment: orange (preferably cold) for each team

When the teams had been formed, Miss Parker blew her whistle again. "All our games and stunts tonight are going to honor the past year," explained Miss Parker. "During 19— (the closing year), Americans shared their surplus food. Our first relay is a Share-the-Food Relay. Will teams line up with players standing shoulder to shoulder and facing in the same direction." Jerry gave each leader an orange and told him to tuck it under his chin. Then he got in line.

"The object of the race is to pass the orange down the line, from player to player, using only 'chin passage,' " explained Miss Parker. "No one must touch the orange with his hands. If the orange falls, the player who was trying to pass it may pick it up and put it under his chin and try again to pass it without using his hands. First team to pass the orange down the line wins. However, the race continues until everyone has passed the orange."

FUND DRIVES

Equipment: two chairs, two clean empty milkbottles, ten pennies

"There were many fund drives in 19—," said Miss Parker. "I'd like each team to choose two Fund-Drive Chairmen."

As the teams were choosing representatives, Jerry placed two identical sturdy chairs in front of the group, with the backs toward the teams.

"During the fund drives," continued Miss Parker, "people put small change into containers for worthy causes." She asked the two FUND-DRIVE CHAIRMEN of the first team to kneel on the chairs, facing the teams. Sarah gave each contestant five pennies, and Jerry put a clean empty milk bottle on the floor in front of each contestant. Each contestant was asked to reach over the back of the chair; and keeping his hand at the level of the chair back, to drop the pennies one by one into the bottle. Everyone counted the pennies that the first two contestants had dropped into the bottle. FUND-DRIVE CHAIRMEN of the other teams took turns dropping pennies into the bottles in the same way. The couple which had put the most pennies into the bottles scored a point for their team.

BARGAIN-SALE CONTEST

Equipment: for each team—table on which to work, identical gift box or book, paper, string

"We all attended bargain sales during 19___," said Miss Parker. "Sometimes our packages looked the worse for wear when we got them home." She asked each team to choose two WRAPPING CLERKS. Jerry set a card table in front of each team, and Sarah put a gift box, paper, and string on each table.

Miss Parker asked each couple to stand behind its table so that their teammates could see them wrap their package and tie it securely.

"Couples must work togeether," explained Miss Parker. *"But—* each partner must keep one hand behind his back and use only his other hand. First couple to get its package wrapped and tied, wins a point for his team. However, all packages must be wrapped."

A RACE AT THE COUNTY FAIR

Equipment: ruler; for each delegate—towel, chair; for each couple —table, dish of ice cream, pair of spoons tied together with 12-inch string

Miss Parker asked each team to choose two delegates to the County Fair. "Remember the eating contests at the 19— Fair?" she asked, as Jerry gave each DELEGATE a towel to put around his neck.

DELEGATES sat in chairs facing their teams. Sarah placed two dishes of ice cream on a table in front of each couple. Jerry measured to make sure that each pair of dishes was 18 inches apart. "Don't move them," he warned. Sarah gave each couple a pair of teaspoons tied together with a 12-inch string.

At a signal, couples began to eat their ice cream, each from his own dish. Couple to finish eating first won for its team. All DELEGATES had to eat all the ice cream in their dishes.

NEWSPAPER HOP

Equipment: several folded newspapers, ruler

"Newspapers printed so much news in 19— that many readers missed some stories. In this contest players must miss the entire newspaper," explained Miss Parker.

Jerry placed several folded newspapers on the floor in a line with 12 inches between each. Miss Parker asked teammates to take partners.

"Each couple will have a turn to race while others watch," explained Miss Parker. "The contest is run this way. A couple stands, side by side, at the head of a line of papers. Each stands on his leg nearest his partner and clutches the other leg with his outside hand. Partners hold hands. At a signal, they hop over the newpapers. If either one touches a news-paper, lets go of his raised leg, topples over, or lets go of the joined hands, the couple is out. A pair from another team tries the hop. Team with the most successful partners scores.

HEADLINES OF THE YEAR

Equipment: for each two players—envelope containing letters of a headline.

Miss Parker asked the group to choose new partners on their own teams. "19— was a great year for headlines," said Miss Parker. "We are going to see how well you can compose headlines. However, in-stead of giving you the story and asking you to write the headline, we'll give you the headline, with the letters cut apart, and ask you to reassemble it."

Jerry gave each couple an envelope containing a headline which had been cut into individual letters. At a signal, each couple tried to arrange the letters to make a headline. When one couple finished, they helped teammates who were having a harder time. First team to complete all its headlines won.

COMMUNITY CO-OPERATION

Equipment: stool; for each team—additional stool and two tongue depressers

"Many community projects were completed in 19— because of co-operation," explained Miss Parker. She asked each team to choose two co-operative representatives.

Jerry placed one stool in front of the teams. He placed a stool for each team 4 feet away from the center stool so that they formed a semicircle around the lone stool. He then placed a paper plate on each team's stool and gave each of the team representatives a tongue de-presser.

"The contest is as follows," explained Miss Parker. "Each contestant puts his tongue depresser in his mouth and grasps his hands behind his back. The object is for teammates to kneel on opposite sides of the plate on their stool, balance the plate on the tongue depressers, lift it, carry it to the vacant stool, and set it on the stool. Remember, no hands!

"Each time players drop the plate, they put it on their own stool and start again. If players give up, they may choose two other players on their team to try. First couple to get a plate on the empty stool wins for their team."

Miss Parker thought for a while that she would have to call time because no couple could get the plate on the vacant stool. However, one couple at last succeeded. What a cheer! All agreed that it had been a contest that was fun to watch as well as try.

INFLATION RACE

Equipment: for each player—balloon and rubber band; for each team—carton to hold balloons

"19— was a year of inflation," announced Miss Parker. Jerry gave each player a balloon and a rubber band. Sarah placed an empty cardboard carton near each team. She asked teammembers to blow up balloons, fasten with rubber bands, and put them in the carton near the team.

Teammates lined up in relay fashion with one player behind the other. Each leader took a balloon from his box and put the balloon between his legs. At a signal, he hopped to a goal on the opposite side of the room and hopped back again. If he broke his balloon, he took another from his team's box and started again. When he returned to his team, he gave his balloon to the next in line who repeated the performance. First team to have everyone hop and return won; but the race continued until everyone had had a turn. Jerry saved the unbroken balloons for BIG BLOW OF THE YEAR.

HAPPY-NEW-YEAR-LOLLIPOP AWARDS

Teammates added their scores for all the races. Sarah gave a Happy-New-Year Lollipop (page 186) to each member of the winning team. Jerry gave undecorated lollipops to other players.

BIG BLOW OF THE YEAR

Equipment—long table, two balloons of different colors

"We all remember the big blow of the year," said Miss Parker, "Hurricane Emily. We are going to have our own big blow."

Players counted off to form two teams. They lined up on opposite sides of a long table. Each player grasped his hands behind his back. Miss Parker placed two balloons of different colors in the center of the table. She assigned one color to each team.

The object of the game was for teammates to blow the opponents' balloon off the table and at the same time keep their own balloon on the table. They had to keep their hands behind their backs. They were allowed to move around the table after the playing started. A point was scored each time a balloon went off the table. Team with ten points lost.

THE OLD YEAR IS DEAD

"By now we all agree that the old year is dead," said Miss Parker. "The question remains, 'How did he die?'" She asked six people to sit in front of the group and demonstrate how the old year died. The stunt is a follows:

The first player says to the person next to him, "The Old Year is dead."

The second player asks, "How did he die?"

The first player says, "Winking an eye." He winks one eye and keeps winking it as the second player says to the person next to him, "The Old Year is dead." The conversation is repeated and the stunt continues until everyone is winking an eye.

The first player then says to the person next to him, "The Old Year is dead."

The second player says, "How did he die?"

The first player says, "Winking an eye and breathing a sigh." He takes one long breath after another and keeps winking his eye. The dialogue and action again go down the line. Soon everyone is blinking and sighing.

The first player says, "The Old Year is dead."

The player next to him asks, "How did he die?"

The first player says, "Winking an eye, breathing a sigh, and trying to fly." He then begins to wink an eye, breathe one sigh after another, and move his arms as if flying. This dialogue and action continues down the line until everyone is winking, sighing and flying.

The first player says, "The Old Year is dead."

The next player asks, "How did he die?"

The first player answers, "Winking an eye, breathing a sigh, trying to fly, and kicking up high." He continues to wink, sigh deeply, wave his arms as if flying, and kick with one foot. The stunt continues until everyone is winking, sighing, flying, and kicking.

"Wow!" said Jerry. "No wonder the Old Year is dead!"

HAPPY-NEW-YEAR REFRESHMENTS

Refreshments were served buffet style: "around the year sandwiches" (an assortment on plates marked "Spring, Summer, Fall, Winter"); date cookies, and Happy-New-Year soft drinks (page 186).

"Happy New Year!" called Jerry as he took the hat from one of the bottles and put it on his head.

"Happy New Year!" echoed his friends as they, too, took hats and donned them.

GENERAL SUGGESTIONS

This party is planned for boys and girls ten years old or older.

Younger children will also enjoy many of the contests, especially at a Cub—or Brownie—Scoutmeeting, or other gathering.

This party may be given by an individual, or two or three friends, in a home with as few as eight players, including the host. Or it may be given by an organization in a social hall or gym.

An End-of-the-Year Party does not have to be given on the last day of the year; does not have to be given at night and does not have to last until midnight. As a rule, two hours is long enough for any party.

However, if your friends want to greet the New Year, and if their parents are willing to call for them, you can plan a party with enough activities to keep them busy and having fun until the agreed time of closing.

This party offers a variety of entertainment. Many of the contests are just as much fun to watch as they are to perform. Try them all before the party to make sure that you understand the directions. If you do not want to do everything, choose events best suited to your group and the place where you are giving the party. HEADLINES OF THE YEAR may be too difficult for some ten-year-olds.

If you are having an afternoon or early evening party, you may not have time for all the events listed. However, if your party is scheduled to last until after midnight, you will need a lot of things to do. It is better to plan too much than too little. If there is time that has not been planned for, play CHARADES (page 185).

Ask an adult to referee the contests. You can decide for yourself if you want to introduce the games and explain them, or if you want the adult to take charge while you take care of props.

GAMES AND STUNTS. In choosing team representatives to take part in stunt contests, be sure that everyone has a turn to perform for his team.

If you do not have an even number for teams, ask some teammates to run twice. Limit teams to six players on a team.

If players especially like a particular relay, stunt, or game, repeat it.

Thread of Life. Decide on how many teams you want for the relays and stunts. Choose a color for each team. Then cut 6-inch lengths of cord of each color so that you will have an equal number for each team.

Big Blow. If your party is large and being held in a social hall have two or more contests going, with a scorekeeper for each game. Play this game as long as players are interested.

The Old Year Is Dead. If your party is small, have guests sit in a circle, with everyone taking part.

Headlines of Year. Cut headlines for each couple into individual letters and place in an envelope. Headlines should not be identical; but they should be clipped from different editions of the same paper in an attempt to insure equal difficulty. Be sure to record the original headline. Maybe no one can assemble it.

CHARADES

There are at least two kinds of charades: word charades and title charades. There are several ways to play either kind. Establish a set of rules and stick to them for the party.

WORD CHARADES: Players are divided into two teams. Each team goes by itself and thinks of a word of more than one syllable to act out. When players get together, the leader tells the number of syllables in the chosen word. The players present a short dialogue for each syllable and one for the entire word.

Teams take turns guessing. Older children can think of and act out more difficult words than younger children. Here are a few simple words.

ribbon	(rib on)	hammock	(ham mock)
napkin	(nap kin)	dandelion	(dandy lie on)
gypsy	(gyp see)	handkerchief	(hand cur chief)

TITLE CHARADES. Players are divided into two groups. One group chooses a title. A member of the team pantomimes it for the other group to guess. First he tells the category. From then on he uses only pantomime. There are certain signals.

The first signal is always the number of words. Player holds up the correct number of fingers. The next signal is word he will pantomime first. He may wish to pantomime the most important word, rather than the first word.

To signal a "little" word (article, preposition, or conjunction) the player crosses his index fingers near the tips. To signal that a word cannot be acted out, player holds hand to ear for "sounds like." He then pantomimes a word that rhymes with word in title.

For example: THE FARMER IN THE DELL. Category: nursery song. Hold up five fingers. Hold up one finger. Cross index fingers. Pantomime farmer working land. Cross index fingers twice. Hold hand to ear to indicate that next word will rhyme with word in title. Pantomime ringing a bell.

185

NEW-YEAR LOLLIPOP

Materials: flat 1½-inch lollipop, scraps of construction paper, paste, rubber band, paper napkin, paper baking cup, ribbon

Fold a paper napkin in half. Fold it over a flat lollipop. Hold in place with a rubber band. Cut out construction paper features and paste them in place. Cut out one side of a paper baking cup so that it looks like a bonnet. Paste the back of the lollipop head on the inside of the baking cup. Wrap a ribbon over the rubber band and tie it in a bow under the chin of the lollipop baby.

HAPPY-NEW-YEAR SOFT DRINKS

Materials: soft drinks in bottles, cellophane tape, construction paper, paper drinking cups, elastic cord

Cut out comic features and tape them onto the soft-drink bottles. You can make funny faces any number of ways and every bottle can have a different face. Make some features three dimensional. For eyes, trace around a quarter and cut out the circles. Fold the top third down for eyebrows. To make a nose, cut out a larger circle. Fold outside edges toward the center so that they form a point at the bottom of the circle. Tape the flat part onto the bottle. For ears, cut out big circles. Fold up two-thirds. Tape the remaining third to the bottle so that ears flap out.

Make a cap for each bottle. Punch holes on opposite sides of a paper drinking cup, near the rim. Insert the ends of a 21-inch piece of elastic cord. Tie big knots in the end of the cord. Put the cup on your head and adjust the length of the cord. Put the hat on a bottle, until it is time for a guest to take it off and use it for a hat.